Caribbean and Southern

Caribbean and Southern

TRANSNATIONAL PERSPECTIVES ON THE U.S. SOUTH

Edited by Helen A. Regis

Southern Anthropological Society Proceedings, No. 38

Christopher P. Toumey, Executive Editor

The University of Georgia Press

Athens and London

Published by the University of Georgia Press
Athens, Georgia 30602

Set in 10.5/13 Adobe Caslon by BookComp, Inc.
Printed and bound by Integrated Book Technology, Inc.

Printed in the United States of America
10 09 08 07 06 C 5 4 3 2 1
10 09 08 07 06 P 5 4 3 2 1

Library of Congress Cataloging-in-Publication Data

Caribbean and Southern : transnational perspectives on the U.S. South / edited by Helen A. Regis.
p. cm. — (Southern Anthropological Society proceedings ; no. 38)
Includes conference papers.
Includes bibliographical references.
ISBN-13: 978-0-8203-2831-7 (cloth : alk. paper)
ISBN-10: 0-8203-2831-6 (cloth : alk. paper)
ISBN-13: 978-0-8203-2832-4 (pbk. : alk. paper)
ISBN-10: 0-8203-2832-4 (pbk. : alk. paper)
1. Ethnology—Southern States. 2. Caribbean Americas—Southern States—Social life and customs. 3. Caribbean Area—Emigration and immigration. 4. Rites and ceremonies—Caribbean Area. 5. Rites and ceremonies—Southern States. 6. Caribbean Area—Social life and customs. 7. Southern States—Social life and customs. I. Regis, Helen A., 1965– II. Series.
GN560.U6C38 2006
306.0975—dc22 2005036671

British Library Cataloging-in-Publication Data available

Contents

Acknowledgments

This book emerges from the collective effort of numerous individuals and several institutions, including the Southern Anthropological Society and the Department of Geography and Anthropology and the College of Arts and Sciences at Louisiana State University. Thanks to Bill Davidson and Craig Colten who supported the project in their capacity as department chair. Mandy Garner Dickerson served as conference coordinator and Michelle Ashton, Eric Dickerson, and Elizabeth Spreng provided crucial assistance during the conference itself. Catherine Benoit and Jay Edwards contributed stimulating papers during the symposium. Elizabeth McAlister presented a paper for a symposium on the Haitian Revolution that provoked much discussion and reflection. Many SAS participants offered illuminating commentaries and questions. Antoinette Jackson provided critical insights that helped me to conceptualize this project early on. Christopher Toumey, Jon Davies, and Gay Gragson expertly guided the manuscript through the editing process. Most of all, this volume would never have come to fruition without the impetus of Miles Richardson, who first suggested that we co-organize the meetings in Baton Rouge, and who encouraged me to organize the key symposium. Richardson's many years of leadership within the Southern Anthropological Society and his scholarship on the U.S. South and Latin America have inspired this effort and his gentle prodding and encouragement helped bring it to fruitful conclusion.

Caribbean and Southern

Introduction

Helen A. Regis

The central theme for the key symposium of the 2003 meetings of the Southern Anthropological Society in Baton Rouge emerged from conversations with friends and colleagues about our conceptualization of the South and its cultural and geographical affinities with other souths—that is, with the global south, as well as with the specific and proximate regions that have long histories of political and economic ties to the United States: South America, Central America, and the Caribbean. The symposium and this volume were inspired by the work of Sylvia Frye and others at the Deep South Regional Humanities Center at Tulane University, as well as by the Center for Southern Culture at the University of Mississippi and the efforts to rethink the U.S. South in light of contemporary cultural history and anthropology, with their emphasis on transnationalism, postcolonial situations, cultural hybridity, border zones, and creolization (see, for example, Glick Schiller and Fouron 2001; McAlister 2003).

All of the contributors to this volume have lived and worked in the South and have long-term research projects in the South, the Caribbean, or both. Their chapters are the result of years, and in some cases, decades, of reflection on the transnational linkages between the plantation complexes of the Caribbean and the South, the cultural continuities between the Caribbean, the South, and Africa, and the structural connections between colonial and postcolonial economies and societies. Some of the authors have personal journeys and biographies that resonate with their research projects. Others use the narratives and life histories of particular elders to show how ancestral roots span the Caribbean and the South.

I can recall being told, soon after my arrival in New Orleans in 1983, that the city is not essentially southern, but rather is the northernmost capital of the Caribbean. As a Franco-American newcomer in New Orleans, I found this geographical decentering compelling. The contemporary pop culture image of the Caribbean evoked ships, not plantations. That is, cruise ships and beaches, rum drinks and spicy foods, reggae and calypso. Yet now this cavalier renunciation of the city's southernness and reclaiming of its Caribbeanness strike me as an ambivalent, complex identity statement. For the city's white residents, it is both a rejection of the most egregious legacies of racial terror and apartheid and simultaneously an effort to embrace a more cosmopolitan, more African-centered geographical affinity.

DISSEMBLING COSMOPOLITAN SOUTHS

The profound transnational connections that shaped the southern United States were silenced during the post-1890 period of racial polarization, reinforcement of existing social hierarchies, and resistance to federalism. Then followed the dismantling of reconstruction and resistance to the judicial and legislative victories of the civil rights movement in 1954 and 1965, respectively. Much of the discourse about the South under the rubric of "local color" literature or regional literature seemed to emphasize the picturesque, the nostalgic, and the colloquial (see Starr 2001). For Louisiana, Alfred Hunt's 1988 book on the consequence of the Haitian revolution for the continental United States marks an important turning point. Social historians began to lay the groundwork for revisionist histories and revisiting contemporary cultural performances through a global lens. Colonial society was reexamined for inaccurate interpretations in light of a social history that seriously considered the experiences of enslaved Africans. Scholars began to consider plantation societies as contact zones between culturally distinct populations. Virginia Domínguez (1986), for example, reconstructed the transformations of racial categories by analyzing court records. And historians like Gwendolyn Midlo Hall found that it was possible, after all, to determine the specific African origins of enslaved people in Louisiana. Hall has warned that studies of colonial societies are inadequate; in Louisiana, such studies require reading knowledge of French and Spanish as well as competence in the paleography of the era. For these reasons, much of the work on nineteenth-century Louisiana has centered on documents that are in English or have been translated, and this has led to late nineteenth-century perspectives being projected anachronistically back on early nineteenth- and eighteenth-century society (see also Domínguez 1986).

Hunt's book carries special meaning for New Orleans: in the early nineteenth century, the city's population doubled through the infusion of Haitian refugees from that island's revolution. Nonetheless, popular discourse in New Orleans about Caribbean connections continued to be marked by silence and denial more than acknowledgement (see Trouillot 1995). The denial of Haitian ancestry among many Louisiana families can be traced to the early nineteenth-century fear of revolution and to the late nineteenth- and early twentieth-century fear among families invested in whiteness of being racially tainted by association with Haiti (see Dubois 2004). In the late twentieth century, as Carole Charles has convincingly argued, a denial of Haitian identity in the United States was rooted in the desire to avoid being "doubly black" (Charles 2003).

In 1998, Marc Morial visited Haiti as one of his first official acts after his inauguration as mayor of New Orleans. This gesture towards the francophone Caribbean and the first black republic in the Western hemisphere bespeaks his initial efforts to brand his mayoral administration with a cosmopolitan vision of the blackness of New Orleans commerce and cultural identities. It was a shocking departure from the self-referential, "only in New Orleans" discourse about the city (see also Smith 2003).

THE ORGANIZATION OF THIS VOLUME

As the essays in this volume collectively demonstrate, any examination of South-Caribbean connections evokes ships and plantations, routes and roots, and an interplay of political economy and cultural performance: agency and coercion, compliance and resistance, revolution and accommodation.

In "From the Chesapeake Bay to the Caribbean Sea and Back," Faye Harrison recenters our narrative on the Caribbean rim, more obvious for the coastal cities of New Orleans and Mobile and Miami, whose geographical intimacy with Cuba and Haiti is well known. Harrison touches on the works of other scholars, but she also advances connections made through decades of personal observation and research. Her own life trajectory reiterates transnational connections made by Afro-diasporic kindred, for instance in the Chesapeake region's historic ties with Jamaica via the performance traditions of John Canoe and the built landscape and architectural features of Atlantic ports, as well as in contemporary developments of heritage tourism.

Paul Farnsworth and Laurie Wilkie bridge historical archaeologies, oral histories, documentary evidence, the analysis of faunal assemblages, and contemporary material culture studies in their consideration of the Bahamian diet. Tacking back and forth between African, southern, and Caribbean foodways, the authors consider the tremendous constraints faced by enslaved Africans and the possible ways in which food cultivation and preparation could constitute an assertion of agency and resilience, expressed through porridge and gravy, homemade beer, and shellfish stews. Their chapter centers on research on Clifton Plantation, founded by American-born British Loyalists who brought enslaved people from the Carolinas and Georgia. "In the foodways of the Loyalist-era Bahamas, we are allowed a glimpse into the process through which multiethnic African communities forge a sense of community identity" (Farnsworth and Wilkie, this volume).

Rosalyn Howard's essay on the Black Seminole diaspora is based on the first ethnohistorical study of the Black Seminole's Caribbean connections (Howard 2002). Military alliances and shared experience of *marronage* by Seminoles and escaped Africans in Florida were rooted in their common opposition to reenslavement, colonization, occupation, and removal. Howard's careful use of oral history, archival documents, and critical readings of published histories recovers an obscured history of the branch of the underground railroad that led South, not North, into the Bahamas.

In her contribution to the volume, Joyce Jackson analyzes the hidden transcripts of women-led religious rituals in Northern Louisiana and Andros Island, Bahamas. Rooted in musical performances, the Easter Rock and Christmas and New Year's Rushin' ceremonies appear, syncretic religious practices sustained in two seemingly unrelated regions of the African Diaspora, yet linked by numerous performative, musical, and theological similarities. Little known outside of these small communities and concealed within larger and better known religious contexts, the Rock and the Rushin' rituals constitute fugitive practices, sustained by women and informed by centuries of cultural resistance to plantation society and dominant religious institutions.

Martha Ward's contribution is part of a larger project that recently appeared as *Voodoo Queen: The Spirited Lives of Marie Laveau* (Ward 2004). Where Jackson and Howard argue for uncovering obscured historical and cultural connections, Ward underlines the distinctiveness of New Orleans Voodoo in comparison with Haitian Vodou. Her work implicitly serves as a warning against sweeping (and ungrounded) claims to connectivities and diasporic connections. The specific social and demographic history of New Orleans means that it often had more intensive cultural influence from Africa than from the Caribbean in the eighteenth century, and more influence from the U.S. interior as migrants from Mississippi and other regions of the rural south migrated in search of refuge from the most extreme regimes of racial terror and in search of economic opportunities in New Orleans. Her work builds on careful historical research, uncovering previously unexploited archival sources (such as close readings of unpublished WPA documents), in combination with oral history and creative, often imaginative reading of contemporary myths and folk archaeologies.

In the final essay, Mark Moberg examines the critical relevance of the concept of environmental racism as advanced by the environmental justice movements in the Caribbean. His chapter bridges a vexed history of environmental racism from genocidal mining practices and sugarcane cultivation to the contemporary practices of massive tourism operations, including all-inclusive resorts and cruise ships as part of South-Caribbean continuities. In contemporary mass tourism, as in colonial sugar plantations, a racially segmented labor force coincides with a political economic structure in which profits are repatriated while environmental costs are borne by the island populations. This pattern is remarkably similar to what has been called environmental racism in the United States, particularly in the critical geographical analysis of the location of chemical plants in low-income, often primarily African American communities.

REFERENCES

Bell, C. 1997. *Revolution, Romanticism, and the Afro-Creole Protest Tradition in Louisiana, 1718–1868.* Baton Rouge: Louisiana State University Press.

Bolster, W. 1998. *Black Jacks: African American Seamen in the Age of Sail.* Cambridge, Mass.: Harvard University Press.

Charles, C. 2003. Being Black Twice. In *Problematizing Blackness: Self-Ethnographies of Black Immigrants to the United States*, ed. P. C. Hintzen and J. M. Rahier, 169–80. New York: Routledge.

Domínguez, V. 1986. *White by Definition: Social Classification in Creole Louisiana.* New Brunswick: Rutgers University Press.

Dubois, L. 2004. *Avengers of the New World: The Story of the Haitian Revolution.* Cambridge, Mass.: Belknap/Harvard University Press.

Glick Schiller, N., and G. Fouron. 2001. *Georges Woke up Laughing: Long-Distance Nationalism and the Search for Home.* Durham: Duke University Press.

Howard, R. 2002. *Black Seminoles in the Bahamas.* Gainesville: University of Florida Press.

Hunt, A. 1988. *Haiti's Influence on Antebellum America: Slumbering Volcano in the Caribbean.* Baton Rouge: Louisiana State University Press.

McAlister, E. 2003. *Rara! Vodou, Power, and Performance in Haiti and Its Diaspora.* Berkeley: University of California Press.

———. n.d. Toward a Comparison of Performance Traditions in New Orleans and Haiti. Paper presented at the symposium on the Legacy of the Haitian Revolution in Louisiana. Organized by Joyce Jackson. Baton Rouge, Louisiana State University.

Smith, F. 2003. Coming of Age in Creole New Orleans. In *Problematizing Blackness: Self-Ethnographies by Black Immigrants to the United States*, ed. P. Hintzen and J. Rahier, 113–28. New York: Routledge.

Starr, F., ed. 2001. *Inventing New Orleans: Writings by Lafcadio Hearn.* Jackson: University Press of Mississippi.

Trouillot, M.-R. 1995. *Silencing the Past: Power and the Production of History.* Boston: Beacon Press.

Ward, M. 2004. *Voodoo Queen: The Spirited Lives of Marie Laveau.* Jackson: University Press of Mississippi.

From the Chesapeake Bay to the Caribbean Sea and Back: Remapping Routes, Unearthing Roots

Faye V. Harrison

BEYOND BOUNDEDNESS

Finding ways to think and raise researchable questions about international and transnational relations between the U.S. South and the Caribbean region is a significant and timely project. The boundedness of culture, society, and nation has been criticized in the conversations anthropologists are having about writing and theorizing against these received notions (e.g., Abu-Lughad 1991). During the current era when social scientists are examining the multiple processes shaping global restructuring and when anthropology is being transformed as a discipline, reconceptualizing and reimagining the South and the Caribbean is more than appropriate. We achieve this goal by deterritorializing the sociocultural and structural features typically associated with the two regions and then reterritorializing and remapping them across the coordinates of interlocking transnational fields of identity, sociocultural dynamics, power, and political economy.

This line of rethinking emerges logically from current trends in anthropology. For me, it also emerges somewhat organically from my lived experience as a southerner born and raised in Norfolk, Virginia; as a Caribbeanist and African diaspora scholar; and as a "minoritized" intellectual. I am a woman of African descent who draws upon both her intellect and intuition and who respects both the power of rigorous empirical observation and the bold license of the imagination. I also acknowledge there is a place for a politics of love in the social production of knowledge (Domínguez

2000). Long before I was inspired by exciting new trends in the field, I had already begun a journey to understand the relationships among culture, power, political economy, and history and the connections, convergences, and parallels that exist between the South and the Caribbean.

RETHINKING WITH INTUITION AND IMAGINATION

I was motivated to wonder about U.S. South–Caribbean connections for a number of reasons. One was purely personal and intuitive. My earliest travel experiences in the Caribbean and Caribbean diaspora, beginning as a high school student in Puerto Rico for a language program, made me intensely aware of a "family of resemblance" with which I felt at home and connected. When I first visited Jamaica, where I have worked intermittently since the late 1970s, I felt an uncanny déjà vu, perhaps based on all I had read and the diasporic consciousness I had cultivated over many years. The feelings Jamaica evoked in me inspired me to wonder whether the Middle Passage ordeal of some of my ancestors had taken them to the Caribbean and, at a later point, transported them to the English colony of Virginia. The birthplace of my paternal family, Virginia was the plantation society from whose plantocracy emerged presidents who helped shape the parameters and identities of what was to become the United States of America. Washington, Jefferson, and others climbed up into national and international prominence on the backs, the bellies, and even the bosoms of enslaved human beings. Was my uncanny sense of having been in Jamaica before like the magical realist journey independent filmmaker Haile Gerima charted for Mona/Shola in "Sankofa"? In that powerful film, the fashion model Mona was returned to her forgotten past in order to be freed from the chains of mental slavery—the neoslavery of a market-centered world that commodifies everything, including black women's bodies and the globally circulated, mass-mediated images of those bodies as seductive objects of consumer desire.

REMAPPING SPACE ACROSS TIME

Beyond the intuitive dimension of my motivation to build a conceptual bridge from the South to the Caribbean, I was also inspired by one of my teachers, the late St. Clair Drake, whose origins were both southern and Caribbean (Baber 1999). Dr. Drake was born in Suffolk, Virginia, of a Virginian mother and a Barbadian father. His father found his way to the southeastern coast of Virginia on one of the many merchant ships that landed there from all over the world. The senior Drake later became a prominent minister and advocate of the Garvey Movement. He made a deep impression on his son, who became a Pan-Africanist Neo-Marxist activist scholar. Before his death in 1990, Drake was an Africanist and African diaspora scholar who laid the groundwork for diaspora studies long before "diaspora" was a buzzword (Drake 1987, 1990). His example and influence have profoundly inspired my work in ways that I never expected when I was his student at Stanford.

During my graduate school years, Drake encouraged me to draw a heuristic map of the Caribbean so that the U.S. South and the littoral areas of Central and South America were included in how I approached the region as a variegated sociocultural and political-economic entity. That mapping of the Circum-Caribbean was enhanced by my consideration of the even more encompassing Plantation America, which extended my examination to the plantation zones of South America. With these overlapping maps, I was able to frame my thinking about southern and Caribbean connections and commonalities in terms of parallel adaptations to "common structural and ecological situations" (Goody 2003) and multidirectional flows of people, culture, knowledge, and commodities across the space of those portions of the Atlantic world. As a student, I was particularly interested in the parallel political economic structures that set the parameters for varying histories and developments of socioeconomic organization, kinship, racial identities, and cultural resistance. It is within this conceptual frame that I continue to approach the interrelations that the Caribbean has long had with the South, specifically the Chesapeake, Carolina/Georgia low country, the Gulf Coast, and Florida, which represent the U.S. South's littoral zone. Because the Chesapeake Bay area is less known for its connections to the Caribbean, I will consider them after highlighting some of the links characterizing the three other subregions.

South Carolina's Caribbean Connections

The interrelations between South Carolina and the Caribbean are integral to understanding the multidimensional social and cultural history of the South, which historians, historical archaeologists, and cultural anthropologists are making clearer. South Carolina was settled by colonists from Britain and Barbados. During the Revolutionary War era, South Carolinian Black Loyalists who fought with the British, either because their masters were pro-British or because they sought their freedom from their pro-national independence Patriot masters, were evacuated along with other

Loyalists from all over the thirteen colonies to other parts of the British Empire and to Great Britain itself. African Americans went to Canada (especially Nova Scotia where my colleague Marilyn Thomas-Houston is conducting ethnohistorical research on this South Carolina diaspora); they also went to Africa, particularly Sierra Leone; and, finally, some made their way to the West Indies, especially to the Bahamas and Jamaica.

Following in the footsteps of historian Monica Schuler (1979), anthropologist John Pulis (Forthcoming, 1999a, b, c) has traced the trajectory of Black Loyalists in Jamaica. Pulis (1999c) is also known for his work on the ethnohistory and theology of Ras TafarI. Thanks to Jamaican anthropologist Barry Chevannes (1994), we know that Ras TafarI's cultural genealogy includes influences from the mid-nineteenth century Great Revival and the cultural resistance of an even earlier generation of syncretic Myalists. Pulis presents evidence that most of the Black Loyalists who made their way to Jamaica were from South Carolina and Georgia rather than from the North. That migration had a significant cultural and political impact, most notably the development of the Native Baptist movement. Pulis scrutinizes the life trajectories of two itinerant ministers, Moses Baker and George Liele, and their participation in the Native Baptist movement, which laid the foundations for Revivalism, a major vehicle for cultural resistance and political contestation. The Native Baptist leadership, in which African Americans figured prominently, "galvanized support against slavery, the slave trade, and the passage of colonial legislation that violated English law" (1999c:12). Native Baptist preachers transmitted a "message of freedom and emancipation" and over time "provided the infrastructure for the 'Baptist War' (1830–32), the single largest slave rebellion to occur in Jamaica" (1999c:31). Messages of freedom and emancipation were also transmitted from the Caribbean to the South. The most powerful instance of this lies in the influence of the slave rebellions that culminated into the Haitian Revolution. Word of the revolution and its commitment to the ideas of equality and liberty traveled far and wide through the idioms of people, both enslaved and free, who cherished freedom.

Louisiana and the Gulf Coast–Caribbean Creole Zone

Of course, South Carolina is only one of many points of departure for illuminating the South's historical relationship with the Caribbean. I call the area of southern Louisiana and the wider Gulf Coast region the French-Creole cultural zone. This region has a history of cultural, economic, and demographic commonalities, connections, and exchanges with the French

Caribbean. Indeed, "from 1718 to 1768, Louisiana was in the hands of the French. [It was in many ways] like its vastly more prosperous sister colony of St. Domingue (now Haiti)" (Domínguez 1986:23). Because of the economic difficulties the colony presented to France, Louis XV passed it on to Spain, whose king was his cousin, in 1768. In 1803, the territory was sold to the United States. During this period of transition, a major transformation was also going on in St. Domingue, soon to become the independent black republic of Haiti. Between 1789 and 1810, heavy waves of refugees streamed into Louisiana from Haiti. Their presence had a marked influence because, as Domínguez states, "they came from an island that excelled in sugar production, had long had large labor-intensive plantations, had been settled much longer than Louisiana, and hence boasted a socially established Creole sector" (1986:102).

But those established Creoles of Haitian and later Louisiana "society" were not the only Caribbean people whose presence had an impact on the sociocultural landscapes of Louisiana and wider Gulf Coast. Not to be forgotten were the enslaved Africans and African Caribbeans who had no choice but to accompany their masters in their great escape from St. Domingue. Those forced immigrants were also cultural and linguistic Creoles, in the etic sense of the term if not in their ethnic identity. Their sensibilities and experiences would lead them to make significant contributions to Louisiana cultural life—most visibly in the realms of cuisine, language, religion, music, and festival arts—such as the culture and art of Mardi Gras. Helen Regis (1999, 2001) has done some interesting and significant work on the cultural politics of festivals, parades, and processions among contemporary working-class African Americans in New Orleans. These Afro-Creole performances, which include the Black Indian masking during Mardi Gras that folklorist and ethnomusicologist Joyce Jackson studies, have tremendous potential for further study. The comparative study of how Amerindians are represented can potentially illuminate the multiple meanings of these stylized figurations in a variety of Caribbean festivals, including Trinidadian Carnival and the Jonkonnu traditions in Jamaica, a number of other English-speaking islands, and, as I shall demonstrate later, the eastern low country or tidewater region of North Carolina.

Because of the racial and cultural politics of identity, speaking what used to be called "Negro Creole" was a marker that made it impossible to claim a Creole identity (Domínguez 1986:211). This speaks to the contested nature of cultural categories and meanings and to the importance of not thinking of culture or cultural areas in homogeneous and power-evasive terms.

The morphology and lexicon of Louisiana Creole resemble those of Haitian Kreyol and are derived in good part from "the language spoken by the [enslaved workers who were forced to accompany the refugees] from St. Domingue who came to Louisiana at the beginning of the nineteenth century. For years it was predominantly a language of rural blacks in southern Louisiana" (1986:210). The public language of white and colored Creoles was French. However, we should distinguish public linguistic performances and personae from actual linguistic practice related to the hidden transcripts of closed quarters. There is ample evidence that the most class-privileged Creoles, especially those of color who were adamant about distinguishing themselves from blacks, regularly engaged in code switching from perfect French in public to Creole in private (1986:211). Code switching of a sort also occurred in the realm of religious expression and practice in which some Louisianians shifted from Roman Catholicism to the mysteries of Voodoo/Hoodoo.

From Florida to the Bahamas

Another important point of embarkation from the South to the Caribbean is Florida's connections to the region through its Spanish colonial ties with the Hispanic Caribbean and the struggles of its African-descended inhabitants for freedom. Historians, historical archaeologists (Deagan and MacMohan 1995, Landers 1990), and anthropological ethnohistorians (Howard 2002) have documented Florida's borderland significance as a site of refuge, *marronage* (i.e., the flight from slavery and the establishment of autonomous settlements by runaways, or maroons), and military defense against Anglo-American expansion and racial slavery. The social and cultural history of Gracia Real de Santa Teresa de Mosé, or Fort Mosé, and other important sites offer important clues about the lived experience of maroons, many of them escapees from South Carolina and Georgia plantations, and about the nature of their alliances with the Spanish and with indigenous peoples, especially those Lower Creeks who came to be identified as Seminoles.

Rosalind Howard's (2002) important research on the Bahamas-bound journey of the Black Seminoles revives an interest that whetted the intellectual curiosity of an earlier generation of researchers. I was introduced to some of them when as an undergraduate I did a research paper on the Red/Black alliance that was a central feature of the Seminole Wars, which spanned from 1817 to 1855, across thirty-eight years of intermittent armed struggle. At that time I was unaware that two early African American anthropologists, Lawrence Foster (1931) and William Willis Jr. (1971), had investigated African and Amerindian contact in the colonial Southeast. In the 1920s and 1930s Foster studied the Black Seminoles, focusing on three of the migratory paths they took from Florida to defend and affirm their freedom in the face of Anglo-American threats to reenslave them. Black Seminoles migrated to Oklahoma (where the majority of conquered aboriginals and their black allies were relocated), Texas, Mexico, and the Caribbean. It took nearly seventy years before an anthropologist followed the fourth path that led to the Caribbean, specifically Andros Island in the Bahamas chain. It took this long, in good part, because the careers of anthropologists like Foster and Willis were limited by the racial economy of anthropological science.

Currently, the Caribbean's connections to Florida are highly visible, especially in South Florida, which has become the gateway to Latin America and the Caribbean. I will have more to say about this later on, but now I wish to discuss at some length the routes and roots that have tied the port city of Norfolk and its Tidewater hinterland in Virginia and eastern North Carolina to the Caribbean, in particular the former British West Indies.

TRAVELING FROM KINGSTON, JAMAICA, TO NORFOLK, VIRGINIA, AND BACK AGAIN

There is one historical embarkation that has led me on a particularly intriguing journey to and from the Caribbean. As I suggested at the outset, this journey has been driven by intuitive, imaginative, and intellectual streams of reflection, particularly those that came together in a 1992 experience in Kingston, Jamaica. That experience was responsible for launching me into a more systematic search for hidden and silenced connections embedded in the narratives and archives of history.

I spent an afternoon with an old friend who had taken me under her wing when I initiated my dissertation research in 1978. She had been one of my key research consultants, but she became much more than that. She was my teacher and fictive kinswoman. In many respects a family of resemblance united us, and that afternoon yet another dimension of our common experience and past became more apparent. That afternoon, fourteen years after we had first met, we walked along the Kingston waterfront, which is walking distance from the impoverished neighborhood where I had met my friend. We walked and talked, reminiscing about years past when she and her sisters, all of whom had emigrated from Jamaica, used to take the ferry from Kingston to Port Royal.

The waterfront beautification, the result of 1980s development efforts to boost the Jamaican economy, contrasted sharply with the rough, tough, and eroding topography of Oceanview, the garrison constituency about which I have written over the years (e.g., Harrison 1997). As I sat and felt the cool breeze from the sea, I thought about the locality's blight and how the already poor community had suffered under the fifteen-year regime of structural adjustment and export-led development. I had made it my job to help document Oceanview residents' "sufferation" and to instantiate the claim that "capitalism gone mad," as Calypsonian social criticism has so aptly put it.

For a moment, the refreshing sea breeze distracted my thoughts from Oceanview's problems. As we gazed out at the sea, I began to think aloud about another waterfront in the town along the southeastern coast of Virginia where I was born. I showed my friend a postcard I kept in a miniature photo album I carried in my bag. The basic layout and design of the two sites were strikingly similar, as though both Norfolk's and Kingston's redevelopment had followed the same architectural and spatial blueprint and were variations on the same theme within an internationalized model of urban planning (Cooper 1999).

The similar downtown landscapes stimulated me to think more about parallels and convergences that place the Chesapeake region of Virginia on the same critical plane with Jamaica and the rest of the Caribbean. Despite my inability to recall any of the schoolbooks I had read ever mentioning Virginia's connections to the West Indies, I eventually came upon information that expanded my understanding of that relationship. Interestingly, in a 1986 encyclopedia set sold in the Louisville, Kentucky supermarket where I shopped, the entry on Norfolk captured my attention, because it stated that the town's "*early growth was based on the West Indies trade and the shipping of products from the plantations of Virginia and North Carolina*" (Funk & Wagnalls New Encyclopedia 1986:136, emphasis mine).

A few years later, an aunt sent me her copy of *Norfolk: Historic Southern Port* (Wertenbaker 1962). She knew that I would be particularly interested in the book because of its detailed discussion of Norfolk's participation in the West Indian trade. Since then, I have come across other work on what Caribbean historian Franklin W. Knight and his colleague, Peggy Liss, have called Atlantic port cities (1991). For instance, historian Jacob Price's (1974, 1991) seminal scholarship on Chesapeake ports examined the place that Baltimore and Norfolk occupied in the development of the Atlantic world. He documented how the low country or Tidewater region of Virginia and Maryland (a state that is technically below the Mason and Dixie line and, therefore, southern) were integrated in British colonial circuits of trade that closely linked them to the British West Indies. Norfolk in particular came to play a specialized role as a seaport town that linked plantation societies in North America and the Caribbean (Price 1974:169).

Because the "mouth of the Chesapeake was considerably closer to the West Indies than was New England," "Norfolk schooners could go all the way to Barbados, or Nevis, or Antigua and back" in a more timely fashion than ships from the larger northern entrepôts, where prices also tended to be dearer (Wertenbaker 1962:35). In the West Indian provision trade, products from the Virginia and North Carolina hinterland (e.g., timber, pitch, tar, barrel staves, hides, tallow, candles, Indian corn, flour, bread, peas, pork, and beef) were sent to Caribbean islands stretching from Jamaica to Barbados in exchange for sugar, molasses, and rum; some pimento, ginger, coffee, and cocoa; and sometimes even slaves to satisfy regional and even national market demand.

Although firmly embedded in the British American political economy, Norfolk merchants did not restrict their commerce to the British West Indies. British mercantilist laws attempted to suppress trade with rival colonial territories; however, those restrictions were regularly circumvented in the interests of profit making—and when tensions between the English and French escalated, the profits were highest. Much of this illegal trade was undertaken with the help of neutral islands like St. Thomas and Curaçao, where Norfolk ships would dock long enough to exchange their cargoes for French sugar and molasses (1962:41). Extensive relations with the French West Indies were developed, and opportunistic trade with Cuba occurred as well.

Historian Thomas Wertenbaker documents that, like Charleston, Norfolk's original settlers included people who had emigrated from the British West Indies during the late seventeenth century (1962:14). By the late eighteenth century, the town's population "numbered among its prominent merchants not only native Virginians and recent Scotch immigrants but Englishmen, Irish, and French West Indians" (1962:88). The latter had sought refuge from the slave uprisings that crystallized into the Haitian Revolution. As compared with northern locales, Virginia appealed to most of these refugees because they could "make use of the . . . slaves they had brought with them" (1962:88). In time, most of the refugees, who numbered in the thousands, dispersed to other parts of the country. Baltimore was probably a popular destination because it was a Catholic stronghold (personal communication with Ina J. Fandrich, Louisiana State University, February 27, 2003). Those French West Indians who remained in Norfolk attempted to restore their fortunes by becoming merchants (Wertenbaker 1962:88).

Historian Tommy L. Bogger (1997) also writes of the French refugees who streamed into Norfolk. He points out that a fleet of 137 vessels sailed into Norfolk in July 1793 bringing free people of color as well as enslaved people, both of whom were initially welcomed along with the white refugees. In time, however, as more refugees streamed into the town, the presence of free French blacks became a problem in a place where policies and laws were designed to restrict the numbers of African descendants who were free. By 1795, the mayor complained to the governor that "the refugees 'generally bring them [slaves and free blacks] in and plead ignorance of the law'" (1997:25, 26). Complaints about French blacks from the islands grew because when they interacted with the local blacks the latter became "impertinent" and hard to control in a situation in which there was "an inadequately armed militia" (1997:26). Haitian blacks were suspected of contributing to the general unrest that led to the Gabriel conspiracy of 1800. The participants of that rebellion "were strongly motivated by the ideals of the French [and Haitian] Revolution[s]"—Liberty, Equality, and Fraternity. The flow of these ideals from Haiti to the U.S. South, mediated by the migration of French Caribbean immigrants and refugees, had a significant impact on the culture of resistance among free and enslaved African Americans.

CARIBBEAN-SOUTHERN U.S. CULTURAL RAMIFICATIONS IN JONKONNU / JOHN CANOE STYLE

The ideas, commodities, and human beings who traveled back and forth between the Chesapeake and the Caribbean impacted the cultural history of the South and the Caribbean. Just as Revolutionary War era Black Loyalists from South Carolina and Georgia influenced cultural and political transformations in Jamaica, the Caribbean immigrants and captives who traveled to southern ports or through them to various destinations beyond Norfolk, Charleston, and New Orleans brought rich cultural cargos with them as well. With those cargoes they provided important inputs into the many local and subregional varieties of southern culture. We may never fully understand the complex sociocultural processes that influenced those cultural continuities and change, but there are clues that we might follow to expand our knowledge and deepen our understanding.

Eastern North Carolina's northernmost reaches were historically a part of the hinterland linked to Norfolk (Westenbaker 1962:30). Up until the 1930s, a street festival tradition of Jonkonnu, John Canoe, or Coonering was a tradition in this part of the state. Jonkonnu is a Christmas and New Year's season festival more commonly found in the Caribbean. Varieties of this secular tradition of masked and parading Jonkonnu bands are found in British-influenced societies such as the Bahamas, Bermuda, Belize, Jamaica, Nevis, and Guyana. The Bahamas tradition appears to share only nomenclature with the Jamaican festival. The latter seems to have clearer connections with Belize's tradition, which has been influenced by the presence of Jamaican migrants in Central America. Today governments are preserving this festival art as a part of their national patrimonies—and, in more economic terms, as part of the colorful cultural heritage component of tourism. In Jamaica, for instance, national festivals and competitions of folk arts that have featured Jonkonnu bands have been organized by either the government or other public institutions (e.g., the leading newspaper, *Daily Gleaner*) at least since the early 1950s as part of the effort to mobilize a common national identity and appreciation of African Caribbean cultural heritage.

In Jamaica, as in eastern North Carolina in years past, Jonkonnu bands made up of wire-screen or mesh-masked and costumed male dancers and musicians traditionally performed in processions usually during Christmas. Now they are more likely to be staged during important state occasions, such as the annual National Festival or Independence Day celebrations in early August. Beginning in the early eighteenth century, these processions of Roots and Fancy Dress bands paraded down the streets moving from house to house or stopping at Great Houses, shops, and the offices of community dignitaries who were expected to give money or food to the performers (Bettelheim 1988:39). The music performed is known as fife and drum music and it consists of two drums, a fife, and a scraper/grater and sometimes a banjo, tambourine, or shaker is added (1988:62).

Roots masquerades include set characters (e.g., Cowhead, Horsehead, Pitchy Patchy, Devil, Warrior, Belly Woman, sometimes Bride, and Amerindian or Wild Indian) each with their own identifiable costume. Some folklorists hypothesize that the Pitchy Patchy costume with its layers of brightly colored strips of fabric has its origins in the vegetal clothing that Maroons wore for camouflage during guerrilla warfare. Jonkonnu bands of the Roots variety have been concentrated in the eastern parishes of the island where neo-African style predominates. Fancy Dress bands, on the other hand, were concentrated in western parishes. Their costumes show stronger European influences. Fancy Dress bands feature the courtly attire of kings, queens, and courtiers embellished by features consistent with a predominant creolized aesthetic. A specific John Canoe or Koo Koo character appears among masqueraders in Fancy Dress parades "dressed up in a mask with long flowing hair . . . carrying a model of a house on his head" (Bettelheim 1988:48). In the roots variety, the Canoe character wears a mask with ox horns or boar tusks.

Because of today's high level of street violence, Jonkonnu performers are hesitant now to parade in public spaces. Consequently, there is no longer a living tradition of neighborhood-based festival participation in urban Jamaica. Moreover, this secular tradition has declined in popularity among younger generations that have found alternative connections with Africa (e.g., through Ras TafarI) and have ambivalent feelings about a festival that originated as a slave celebration that, among other things, entertained white masters. Performances now tend to be staged and sponsored by institutionalized patrons such as the Jamaican Cultural Development Commission.

In eastern North Carolina, the John Canoe or Coonering procession has been described as all male, with fiddles, banjos, and homemade instruments including lard can drums. The procession would stop at the kitchen doors of big white-owned farms where John Cooners expected to be given money or food. One account by an uncle of an alumnus of the University of Tennessee's graduate program described waking up early Christmas or New Year's Day to the "raucous sound of music." The setting for that incident was fifteen miles southeast of Fayetteville (pers. com. via email with Brett Riggs, February 3, 2003).

Accounts of similar Christmas season parades of masked revelers are found in the journal *North Carolina Folklore*, which documents the survival of a Pitchy Patchy style. According to one article, "on Christmas Eve, John Kuners, Negroes, went about singing, dressed in tatters with strips of gay colors sewn to their garments. All were men, but some dressed as women. They wore masks. . . . They collected pennies at each house" (Walser 1971:161). Descriptions of the John Canoe figure indicate that "he wears a mask. . . . He goes through a variety of pranks [and] is accompanied by a crowd of [Negroes] who make noise and music for his worship John Kooner" (1971:162). John Canoe is described as a ragman with two great ox horns or branching deer horns "attached to the skin of a raccoon" arranged over his head and face, leaving openings for his eyes and mouth. A second figure was described as the "best looking darkey of the place" who wears his Sunday best (1971:162).

In some parts of eastern North Carolina, a reinterpreted form of "the custom survived for a while among whites who seem not to have been aware of its Negro origin" (1971:169). Joncooners "were an established part of the Christmas observance." Young men would dress up in "outlandish" costumes, often women's attire, and wear "scare-faces." In minstrel style they would also blacken their faces or if they preferred not to, they would wear clown costumes and facial masks. Coonering would begin as early as five o'clock on Christmas morning, waking up residents with Christmas carols and other songs.

This past practice seems to have striking similarities with the recent black-face antics of white fraternities on southern college campuses (e.g., Auburn University and the University of Tennessee, Knoxville) in which white males have paraded around frat houses or the streets wearing black face, sometimes Afro wigs, and pillow-stuffed bellies under women's dresses, making offensive statements about irresponsibly fertile welfare queens and African Americans in general. Can we think of these instances as a contemporary form of "coonering," especially when performed in the South?

The origins of the Jonkonnu term are sometimes attributed to "the French phrase *gens inconnus* which means "the unknown people," a reference to the masking . . . of festival celebrants" (Howard, forthcoming:21). Sociologist Ira de A. Reid (1942) offered an alternate explanation. In his view the origins of the east Carolinian festival are found in a retained Africanism traceable to West Africa. He claimed that there was an early eighteenth century chief named John Connu. Supposedly, a festival he originated on the Guinea Coast was brought to the West Indies and later diffused to North Carolina, "whose more wealthy plantation owners had continuous commerce with the islands" (Walser 1971:172). Some research suggests that commerce with Jamaica in particular gave rise to east Carolina's Jonkonnu tradition, a virtually forgotten tradition that is now being revived in limited contexts of public programming and cultural heritage tourism.

The North Carolina Humanities Council has played an important role in promoting scholar-community collaborations for researching local histories of Jonkonnu. This research has fed into the revitalization of Jonkonnu as an element of cultural heritage tourism. A couple of fairly recent examples of reviving or recreating Jonkonnu are the following events advertised or reported on the Internet. Among the many Christmas festivities featured in New Bern, North Carolina, since 2000 is Tryon Palace's reenactment. An advertisement published in 2001 stated the following:

> Making a return appearance for Christmas 2001 is Tryon Palace's Jonkonnu Celebration, the colorful African American holiday procession that was popular in Eastern North Carolina during the 19th century but had disappeared by the start of the 20th century. When Tryon Palace Historic Sites & Gardens brought Jonkonnu back to life last Christmas, it proved to be such a crowd-pleaser that the Tryon Palace Jonkonnu troupe was later invited to reprise the celebration at Gov. Easley's inauguration in Raleigh. The Jonkonnu ceremony, a blend of West African and English traditions, features a festive parade of elaborately costumed singers, dancers and musicians. Free performances will take place between at 6 and 8 p.m. on each of the candlelight evenings, Dec. 14, 15, 21, and 22. (Hall 2001)

The celebration was advertised with these words of invitation to the public: "Costumed singers, dancers and musicians will [recreate] Jonkonnu, an African-American yuletide tradition unique to eastern North Carolina, along Pollock Street in New Bern at 6 p.m. and 8 p.m. today and Saturday. The festive procession will wind from house to house in the town's historic district, bringing to life a 19th-century blend of African, Caribbean and English customs. Free. Call 1-800-767-1560" (Daily Reflector 2001).

TWENTIETH AND TWENTY-FIRST CENTURY CONFIGURATIONS OF CARIBBEAN–SOUTHERN U.S. CONNECTIONS

The continuous commerce between various southern locales and the Caribbean constituted a transcolonial and later transnational sociocultural field that is a rich site for unburying and retrieving the silenced history that denies Southerners and Caribbean people the historical consciousness, memory, and knowledge that is part of their overlapping cultural heritage. The Upper South has been especially neglected and, for that reason, I feel motivated to fill that gap. Other gaps, however, need to be addressed as well, and a number of historians and anthropologists have been pursuing important research directions that give voice to silenced chapters of the convergent cultural and socioeconomic history of the South and Caribbean.

Beyond questions of history, twentieth and now twenty-first century developments, both parallel adaptations to similar structural situations and direct interchanges between the two regions, encourage us to situate the

Caribbean and South within overlapping transnational fields. Anthropologists such as Tony Whitehead, Willie Baber, and myself—among others—are seeing to it that some of the concepts and theoretical discourses that were developed originally in the context of Caribbean studies and studies of plantation societies elsewhere are allowed to "travel" to the research agendas and social analysis being pursued in the South and the southern diaspora. Whitehead (1986, 1997) is an exemplary instance of someone whose analysis of U.S. situations in Washington, D.C., and Baltimore draws on tools honed through his earlier Caribbean research on family, fertility, and men. His approach to African American lower class masculinity and its influence on health-related behaviors, particularly those affecting the incidence of HIV/AIDS, draws upon a model of masculinity he developed through a constructive critique of Peter Wilson's (1973) reputation-respectability typology. Whitehead has also used his model of socially balancing the values and practices of respectability and reputation in thinking in new ways about his own experiences as an African American male from rural Tidewater Virginia. His Chesapeake subregional background may only be incidental to his work as an anthropologist, but I find it interesting that a fellow Virginian is drawing these kinds of connections and bringing interrogations of Caribbean life so close to home. He is an intellectual courier who has accepted the responsibility for fashioning and applying a repertoire of border-crossing, traveling theory.

In addition to cultural constructs of manhood and womanhood and their embeddedness in intersecting hierarchies of race, class, and sexuality, other topics and themes amenable to this traveling theory approach include: kinship, mating, household organization, and livelihood strategies; the social construction of race, especially in contexts such as New Orleans and Charleston where tripartite classification systems have contested the Anglo-dominant bipolarity, and in the many areas of the south, parts of Virginia and North Carolina included, where triracial communities have defiantly claimed identities otherwise precluded by the "one drop rule"; the Caribbeanization of southern places through new waves of immigration; the dual and conflicting politics of reception for various categories of Caribbean refugees, e.g., Haitians and Cubans, and the interplay between domestic and foreign policy concerns; the emergence of new Caribbean-inspired religious identities and the search for "Africa"; economic and environmental developments influenced by U.S. policy-induced conditions in the Caribbean; and threats to the viability of small farmers and considerations of the transnational relevance of the concepts crafted for agrocapitalism and reconstituted

Caribbean peasants and proletarians. I will discuss four of these possibilities in greater detail in the sections that follow. Because debates concerning kinship, marriage, and sexual politics have been intense in both Caribbean and African American studies, I will treat this particular topic in some detail.

The Racial and Class Politics of Stratified Kinship and Marriage

Anthropological studies of kinship and social organization have elaborated parallel themes for Caribbean and African American studies. When I was a graduate student I attempted to address these overlapping concerns by using the concept of Plantation Society as an analytical frame that allowed me to put the U.S. South and the English-speaking Caribbean in particular on the same page. The prevalence, for instance, of matrifocality in social organization, patterns of cooperative child raising within consanguineal groupings (most commonly organized around ties among maternal blood lines), and high rates of visiting relationships and consensual sexual unions were issues or "problems" that sociologists and anthropologists felt they had to explain. Were they pathological symptoms of attenuated families, part of the legacy of slavery, which forced families apart, reducing them to mother-child dyads? Or was an alternative African-inspired cultural logic at work that organized primary relations around mothers and their kin, both female and male, and placed greater cultural emphasis on consanguineality than on conjugal ties (Sudarkasa 1996)? These adaptations emerged in different plantation and peasant society environments where migration from family land—be it peasant small holdings barely capable of sustaining a household or sharecropper or tenant farming plots—was impelled to reproduce households, domestic networks, and families left back home in the country. Marked similarities, parallels, and instances of human agency were responding creatively yet restrictively to similar structures of power and political economy, structures with a shared history in many respects but also divergent histories marked by particularities specific to different social formations, different social orders.

R.T. Smith's (1987) and Lisa Douglass's (1992) analyses of the dual marriage system have a number of parallels with Allison Davis et al.'s (1941) analysis of kinship and mating across lines of caste and class in Natchez, Mississippi in the 1930s. Anthropologists have not theorized explicitly about southern kinship in terms of connections between whites and blacks. These have been neglected, taboo subjects since *Deep South* (Davis et al. 1988). My reading of that classic ethnography leads me to think that its analysis represents an embedded theorizing about a system of stratified kinship and mating in which men of the privileged caste were granted the prerogative of marrying within their own caste while having the license to have long- or short-term relationships with concubines from the lower caste. In other words, sociocultural principles operated that permitted white men to have their cake and eat it, too, in the midst of a repressive Jim Crow climate in which antimiscegenation (or resistance to legitimate race crossing) was legally codified. The gender bias and sexual politics of this culture of racism was only a more hypocritical, contradictory, and repressive version of the variant that Smith characterized in his model of the Caribbean's dual marriage system. In this stratified but in some significant ways unified system, patriarchal prerogatives, constructs of masculinity, matrifocality, and interhousehold cooperation are manifested across social lines but in class-specific ways.

Thanks to Douglass's explanation, we have a better understanding of how interlocking hierarchies of gender, color, and class operate to constitute the shared cultural system that so many sociologists and anthropologists have failed to discern. Smith did us a real service by treating the double standard and masculine privilege as an issue worthy of scrutiny. He explained how the de facto polygyny of upper-class men is informed by the same cultural system that informs the reputational behavior of lower-class African Caribbean men whom, since Peter Wilson (1973), have been the focus of considerable debate in the literature. Masculine virility and strength exhibited in sexual conquests and managing multiple baby-mothers simultaneously are valued as long as they are not taken too far, as Whitehead tells us. However, social balance is also valued; therefore, when men end up not being able to contribute to the livelihood of their children, they are considered weak and perhaps wicked. This kind of demonstration of virility is also expected among middle-class and upper-class men, who in achieving social balance and some measure of respectability are expected to own up to their exploits and contribute to the welfare and perhaps the social mobility of their outside children.

In the Caribbean, the climate has been rather promiscegenation, with ideologies of mixedness defining national identities. "Out of many, one people" is the national motto in Jamaica, emphasizing its multiracial heritage. However, as many race-conscious Jamaicans point out, 95 percent of the population is black, so why overstate the presence of Chinese, Indians, Lebanese, Germans, and British-descended whites when since the 1930s the Ras TafarI have been insisting that Ethiopia—Africa—must be recognized as home?

The kinship and gender constructs that ethnographic research mapped in Mississippi (Davis et al. 1941) and decades later in the Chesapeake city of Baltimore among lower-class black men (Whitehead 1997) are not limited to those sites. These constructs are relevant to studies of other parts of the South and its migration-mediated diasporas in northern, midwestern, and West Coast cities.

Besides kinship, marriage, and the cultural politics of masculine sexual prowess, there are other issues germane to the kind of research agenda I sketch here. I will raise some points about three of them before I conclude.

The Migration of African-Caribbean Orishas and Loas

We should pay more attention to recent migrations to the South and the consequent cultural and religious identities they form, such as the Yoruba-inspired communities in South Carolina, Atlanta, and New Orleans. Cuban-American anthropologist Beatriz Morales (1995) has written insightfully about the arrival of the Yoruba movement in the United States and its dispersion into the South. This dispersion began with the migration of Cubans, particularly Afro-Cubans, to the United States, where they continued their practice of Santería and its more traditional Yoruba form called Lucumí.

In the midst of the black movement of the 1960s and 1970s, Santería was changed as non-Cuban blacks were attracted to it as a purportedly more authentic African form of religiosity. In northern urban settings, a new syncretized Orisha-Voodoo emerged that placed greater emphasis on African cultural identity and less emphasis on the Roman Catholic saints that represented, in the new converts' view, the Western Judeo-Christian framework. This Afrocentric negation of Santería's syncretic relationship to Christianity created tensions between Orisha-Voodoo and the followers of Santería. That conflict led the proponents of Orisha-Voodoo to establish a new base in rural South Carolina. That base became the Oyotunji Village, a recreation of an African village. The Oyotunji settlers chose South Carolina rather than upstate New York because of their belief that the South, as the historic Black Belt, was more conducive to building African culture. Religious specialists initiated in Oyotunji later established Yoruba centers elsewhere, such as the one in Atlanta. Morales shows how the Orisha-Voodoo religion is expanding to accommodate a shift back to a more Santería-oriented form because of Atlanta's growing multicultural population. As more Latinos joined the religion, the temple established closer ties with the Santería community. As a consequence, the temple now initiates its adherents into either of the two traditions and both groups "treat each other as equals" (Morales 1995:130).

The Cuban Embargo, NAFTA, and Sugar Politics in Florida

Anthropologist Max Kirsch (2003) has examined economic developments in the Florida Everglade zone that are influenced by U.S. foreign policy and conditions in the Caribbean, which are mutually constitutive. He demonstrates that the sugar industry based in the state of Florida has benefited from the U.S. embargo against Cuba, whose sugar cannot be imported here. The embargo created an opening for Cuban émigrés to build an enclave in Florida and lobby for protection from NAFTA's free trade regulations up until 2008.

Sugar production, so central to the economic history of the Caribbean, has expanded in Florida to the detriment of the state's wetlands, which have been drained. Sugar producers, especially the Cuban émigrés who restored their business interests with U.S. protection, became a major force in national and Florida politics (Kirsch 2003:114–15), influencing foreign and domestic environmental policies. Until 2008, when the NAFTA exemption may be lifted, Cuban American–controlled sugar production will continue to be subsidized by the U.S. government. Both environmental and labor groups have taken the industry to court for polluting the environment and for mistreating and jeopardizing the health of migrant workers, some of whom are from the Caribbean (e.g., Haitians). Because of the vulnerable immigration status of the workforce and "the concern (and threats) about the possible loss of jobs," health conditions had not received the attention they deserved before the recent litigation (Kirsch 2003:104). In response to the lawsuits, sugar companies have mechanized harvesting, relegating most workers to planting and to off-season migration to work on citrus farms in other areas.

The Everglades Agricultural Area is the locus not only for sugarcane production but also for several other crops, among them "tomatoes, beans, lettuce, sugar beets, watermelons . . . and Chinese vegetables" (Kirsch 2003:106). Supporting the production of these primary commodities are "strong fluid communities [of African and Native Americans,] Mayan-speaking Guatemalans [and] Caribbean immigrants [which] exist beyond the realm of the production line" (Kirsch 2003:106). These communities challenge the organizational capacity of social service agencies whose conspicuousness and diversity belie their ability to meet basic needs and ameliorate local conditions. Through resilient ties of kinship and local organization, both American-born and immigrant workers negotiate the demands of their everyday lives in a nexus of culture, power, and identity that is situated where the local and transnational intersect.

Farmers and/or Peasants?

Some parallel problems might be better understood if we examine them with bifocal vision, that is, by asking questions that have relevance for both Caribbean and southern contexts and that enable us to compare and contrast those cases. For instance, the work on the categorization, struggles, and negotiations of Caribbean peasants raises interesting questions that might fruitfully be applied to the daunting situation faced by the South's small farmers, particularly black farmers who represent an endangered species and are mobilizing to combat their plight. Being neither peasant nor proletarian (Frucht 1971) seems to be the growing predicament for the variety of rural folk who might be categorized as farmers—from sharecroppers to tenants to landowners of varying scales.

Willie L. Baber has raised this question based on his work on the struggles of North Carolina farmers to survive agribusiness's encroachments on their land and the degradation of their environment (pers. com., November 21, 2000). His perspective on what he has observed in Halifax County in the northeast of the state has been influenced by his earlier work in rural Martinique on peasant production undergoing change in a globalizing economy (Baber 1988). Whether the concept of "peasant," particularly how it has been formulated for Caribbean contexts, is appropriate for the South or not, situating the agricultural work of southern smallholders along side Caribbean peasants for the sake of comparison and contrast could add dimensions and nuances that otherwise would not be part of the discussion.

The importance of comparing and contrasting cases from the southern United States and the Caribbean is reflected in the parallel histories of the small farmers concerned. For instance, during the antebellum period, South Carolina and Georgia had protopeasant formations with concomitant systems of internal marketing similar to those developed in Jamaica and other parts of the Caribbean.

The experience of peasants and proletarians are variable rather than categorical, essentialist realities. The boundary between these categories is ambiguous and conditioned by a hybrid experience. Richard Frucht's (1971) writing on the rise and demise of peasants in Nevis presents a useful perspective on these matters. A reconstituted peasantry on the order of what emerged in the Greater Antilles and in certain eastern Caribbean contexts did not develop in Nevis. The main reasons were the island's small size and the lack of open areas uncontrolled by plantations.

According to Frucht, "the word 'peasant' is not to be here understood as a categorical concept describing a subculture or kind of community. It is not to be so understood because the so-called peasantry of Nevis has always been inextricably bound to the plantation system or to some other system of wage labor in more than an occasional sense. This is an artifact of geography, of economic history, and of the economic and political predominance of the industrial, colonial power" (Frucht 1971:99).

He went on to argue that:

> in Nevis, whereas there is a peasant-like means of production, which includes cultivation of small plots with the use of household labor and traditional manual technology, the relations of production are proletarian . . . based on the sale of labor for wages either paid in cash or in kind, and the latter through systems of sharecropping, farming out and under conditions of male labor emigration. Finally, the existence together and in alteration of seemingly disparate means and relations of production is an adaptations of the vicissitudes of a marginal economy. (Frucht 1971:99)

He described how, over time, the predominance of sharecropping and farming out declined and the big plantations were sold to speculators who in turn sold subdivided plots to smallholders. For a short while after World War II, a peasant adaptation was reconstituted; however, years later emigration opportunities expanded as tourism and concomitant construction and service jobs emerged as a focus of economic life. By the 1960s and 1970s, dependence on remittances had replaced agricultural production as the livelihood strategy for roughly 70 percent of the adult population, whose peasant holdings were used for garden vegetables or as an asset to be used for "insuring bank loans for further emigration" (Frucht 1971:102).

The declining viability of small holdings as units of agricultural production and the growing dependence on alternative sources of income, primarily service jobs and remittances from transnational relatives, are issues similar to those affecting many rural communities in the southern United States. These communities are undergoing transformations influenced in part by their own specific histories of sharecropping, small holdings, migration to the urban North, and now, in the context of deindustrialization and economic restructuring, return migration as Carol Stack's (1996) research documents.

Melissa Hargrove (2005) shows how African Americans, specifically those with Gullah/Geechee identities, in South Carolina's and Georgia's Sea Islands are being circumscribed and, in many instances, altogether displaced by resort and tourism development. Similar to the situation in the Caribbean, tourism is capitalizing on the culturally distinctive heritage of sweet grass basket making and Gullah language-based performances, while real estate developers are rapidly expanding the construction of hotels, golf courses, and wealthy gated communities that symbolically "reinvent" and romanticize the plantation. Local activist organizations are contesting the alienation of the Gullah from their traditional homes and means of livelihood. According to one grassroots organization, the Gullahs' human rights are at stake and this grievance has been expressed in a United Nations forum (Hargrove 2000).

TRAVELING ACROSS INTERLOCKING TRANSNATIONAL FIELDS: CONCLUDING REMARKS

In this essay, I have related aspects of the life history of my efforts to begin rethinking the transcolonial and transnational connections that have mutually constituted the two regions we know as "the South" and "the Caribbean." I have tried to provide a sense of how I am attempting to remap the cultural and structural space in which these two zones of social analysis and theory conjoin and interpenetrate by using a cartography that is responsive to the passage of time. I have revealed aspects of my own personal journey to transcend the structured and enforced silences of the historical past and present so that more people of the South and the Caribbean might have the choice to claim the migrations, the evacuations, the commodity chains, the plantations, the small holdings, the Maroon wars, the Baptist War, the systems of kinship stratified by color and class, the new religions, the Creole languages, the Christmas and pre-Lenten festivals, the masks, and the musical revelry that has bound us together despite the big waters that appear to separate us. My listening beyond the silences has been aided not only by conventional intellectual tools, but also by some measure of intuition and imagination, inspired by a politics of love (Domínguez 2000).

Growing up in Norfolk, Virginia may have predisposed me to study anthropology and to travel in search of, and later with, theoretical cargo whose value is transferable. Norfolk's relationship with major waterways and its openness to the Atlantic World, especially the Caribbean, made it an appropriate base of embarkation and disembarkation in my journey to and from, back and forth between the Chesapeake Bay and the Caribbean Sea, between my imagination and analytic intellect, between the temporal landscapes of ancestral presence and the cultural geography of present-day diasporas and their constituent diasporas. To and from, back and forth, remapping travel routes and unburying cultural roots as I go about my journey (Hall 1999:5).

On the evening of February 22, 2003 as I was working on the original draft of this essay, the Trumpet Awards Ceremony, a program to celebrate African American heroes and sponsored by a number of major corporations (e.g., Delta Airlines, Coca Cola, GM, Kroger, Miller Brewing Company, and Anheuser Busch), was broadcast on the Turner Broadcasting System's superstation. The Right Honorable Perry Gladstone Christie, Prime Minister of the Bahamas (who happens to belong to a Jonkonnu group), was presented a Global Achievement Award. In his thank-you speech, he reminded the largely African American audience that Bahamians and African Americans share a great many things in common and that the Bahamas nation has contributed to African American achievements, beginning, of course, with Sidney Poitier. He ended with the following insightful words, which are relevant to the themes of this essay, especially as those themes relate to the African diaspora. He said:

> An expanse of water separates us, but an expanse of water should never divide us. One family insoluble under God.

ACKNOWLEDGMENTS

This was originally a keynote address delivered at the annual meeting of the Southern Anthropological Society in February 2003 in Baton Rouge, Louisiana. I would like to thank Helen Regis for inviting me and encouraging me to distill ideas I have been rehearsing for many years. I would also like to thank Brett Riggs for his conversations during his years at the University of Tennessee-Knoxville and, more recently, his reply to my email request that he confirm the story he told me about Jonkonnu in eastern North Carolina. That bit of information shared several years ago reinforced my wish to remap the South's ties to the Caribbean region. Pearl Hamilton Harper, my dear aunt, has been such a gem over the years. The history book she gave me quite a while ago was an important turning point in my knowledge about the place our hometown occupies in the wider Atlantic World. Another useful book, one focused on free black Norfolkians, was a gift from my uncle, the late Dr. Herbert Marshall, whose enthusiasm for my scholarship I will always appreciate.

REFERENCES

Abu-Lughod, L. 1991. Writing Against Culture. In *Recapturing Anthropology: Working in the Present*, ed. R. Fox, 137–62. Santa Fe: School of American Research Press.

Baber, W. 1988. *The Economizing Strategy: An Application and Critique*. New York: Peter Lang.

———. 1999. St. Clair Drake: Scholar and Activist. In *African American Pioneers in Anthropology*, ed. I. Harrison and F. Harrison, 191–212. Urbana: University of Illinois Press.

Bettelheim, J. 1988. Jonkonnu and Other Christmas Masquerades. In *Caribbean Festival Arts: Each and Every Bit of Difference*, ed. J. Nunley and J. Bettelheim, 39–83. Seattle: University of Washington Press in association with the Saint Louis Art Museum.

Bogger, T. 1997. *Free Blacks in Norfolk, Virginia: The Darker Side of Freedom*. Charlottesville: University Press of Virginia.

Chevannes, B. 1994. *Rastafari: Roots and Ideology*. Syracuse: Syracuse University Press.

Cooper, M. 1999. Spatial Discourses and Social Boundaries: Re-imagining the Toronto Waterfront. In *Theorizing the City: The New Urban Anthropology*, ed. S. Low, 377–99. New Brunswick: Rutgers University Press.

Daily Reflector. Jonkonnu celebration. December 20–26, 2001. http://www.reflector.com/fea...002/12/19/1040356116.01917.8510.0574.html (accessed February 24, 2003).

Davis, A., B. Gardner, and M. Gardner. 1988 [1941]. *Deep South: A Social Anthropological Study of Class and Caste*. Los Angeles: Center for African American Studies.

Deagan, K., and D. MacMahon. 1995. *Fort Mosé: Colonial America's Black Fortress of Freedom*. Gainesville: University Press of Florida.

Domínguez, V. 1986. *White by Definition: Social Classification in Creole Louisiana*. New Brunswick: Rutgers University Press.

———. 2000. For a Politics of Love and Rescue. *Cultural Anthropology* 15(3): 361–93.

Douglass, L. 1992. *The Power of Sentiment: Love, Hierarchy, and the Jamaican Family Elite*. Boulder: Westview Press.

Drake, S. 1987, 1990. *Black Folk Here and There: An Essay in History and Anthropology*. 2 vols. Los Angeles: Center for Afro-American Studies, University of California.

Foster, L. 1931. Negro-Indian Relations in the Southeast. PhD diss., Columbia University.

Frucht, R. 1971 [1967]. A Caribbean Social Type: Neither "Peasant" nor "Proletarian." In *Black Society in the New World*, ed. R. Frucht, 98–104. New York: Random House.

Funk and Wagnalls New Encyclopedia. 1986. Norfolk, 135–36. Rand McNally.

Goody, J. 2003. Globalization and the Domestic Group. *Urban Anthropology and Studies of Cultural Systems and World Economic Development* 32(1):41–56.

Hall, M. 2001. Tyron Palace Christmas. Kinston Free Press. Electronic document, http://www.kinston.com, accessed February 24, 2003.

Hall, S. 1999. Thinking the Diaspora: Home-Thoughts from Abroad. *Small Axe* 6:1–18.

Hargrove, M. 2000. Marketing Gullah: Identity, Cultural Politics, and Tourism. MA thesis, Department of Anthropology, University of Tennessee, Knoxville.

———. 2005. Reinventing the Plantation on Gullah-Contested Landscape: Gated Communities and Spatial Segregation in the Sea Islands. PhD diss., Department of Anthropology, University of Tennessee, Knoxville.

Harrison, F. 1997. The Gendered Politics and Violence of Structural Adjustment. In *Situated Lives: Gender and Culture in Everyday Life*, ed. L. Lamphere, H. Ragoné, and P. Zavella, 451–68. New York: Routledge.

Howard, R. 2002. *Black Seminoles in the Bahamas*. Gainesville: University Press of Florida.

———. Forthcoming. Yoruba in the British Caribbean: A Comparative Perspective on Trinidad and the Bahamas. In *The Yoruba Diaspora in the Americas,* ed. T. Falola and M. Childs. Bloomington: Indiana Press.

Kirsch, M. 2003. The Politics of Exclusion: Place and the Legislation of the Environment in the Florida Everglades. *Urban Anthropology and Studies of Cultural Systems in World Economic Development* 32(1):99–131.

Knight, F., and P. Liss, eds. 1991. *Atlantic Port Cities: Economy, Culture, and Society in the Atlantic World, 1650–1850*. Knoxville: University of Tennessee Press.

Landers, J. 1990. Gracia Real de Santa Teresa de Mosé: A Free Black Town in Spanish Colonial Florida. *American Historical Review* 95(1):9–30.

Morales, B. 1995. Returning to the Source: Yoruba Religion in the South. In *Religion in the Contemporary South: Diversity, Community, and Identity*, ed. O. Kendall White Jr and D. White, 124–30. Southern Anthropological Society Proceedings, no. 28. Athens: University of Georgia Press.

Price, J. 1974. Economic Function and the Growth of American Port Towns in the Eighteenth Century. *Perspectives in American History* 8:123–86.

———. 1991. Summation: The American Panorama of Atlantic Port Cities. In *Atlantic Port Cities: Economy, Culture, and Society in the Atlantic World, 1650–1850*, ed. F. Knight and P. Liss, 262–76. Knoxville: University of Tennessee Press.

Pulis, J. 1999a. "Citing [Sighting]-Up": Words, Sounds, and Reading Scripture in Jamaica. In *Religion, Diaspora, and Cultural Identity: A Reader in the Anglophone Caribbean*, ed. J. Pulis, 337–401. Amsterdam: Gordon and Breach.

———, ed. 1999b. *Moving On: Black Loyalists in the Afro-Atlantic World*. New York: Garland.

———. 1999c. The Jamaican Diaspora: Moses Baker, George Liele, and the African American Migration to Jamaica. Paper presented in the School of American Research Advanced Seminar, "From Africa to the Americas: New Directions in Afro-American Anthropology," April 11–15, 1999. Santa Fe: New Mexico.

———. (Forthcoming). "Important Truths and Extravagant Peruilities": Piety, Subversion, and the Anabaptist Church of Jamaica. In *Afro-Atlantic Dialogues: Anthropology in the Diaspora*, ed. K. Yelvington, 193–210. Santa Fe: School of American Research Press.

Reed, I. 1942. The John Canoe Festival: A New World Africanism. *Phylon*, Fourth Quarter: 349–70.

Regis, H. 1999. Second lines, Minstrelsy, and the Contested Landscapes of New Orleans Afro-Creole Festivals. *Cultural Anthropology* 14(4):472–504.

———. 2001. Blackness and the Politics of Memory in the New Orleans Second Line. *American Ethnologist* 28(4):752–77.

Schuler, M. 1979. Myalism and the African Religious Tradition in Jamaica. In *Africa and The Caribbean: Legacies of a Link*, ed. M. Crahan and F. Knight, 65–79. Baltimore: Johns Hopkins University Press.

Smith, R. 1987. Hierarchy and the Dual Family System in West Indian Society. In *Gender and Kinship: Essays toward a Unified Analysis*, ed. J. Collier and S. Yanagisako, 163–96. Stanford: Stanford University Press.

Stack, C. 1996. *Call to Home: African Americans Reclaim the Rural South*. New York: Basic Books.

Sudarkasa, N. 1996. Interpreting the African in African American Family Structure. In *The Strength of Our Mothers: African and African American Women and Families: Essays and Speeches*, 123–41. Trenton: Africa World Press.

Walser, R. 1971. His Worship the John Kuner. *North Carolina Folklore* 19(4): 160–72.

Wertenbaker, T. 1962 [1931]. *Norfolk: Historic Southern Port*. 2nd ed. Durham: Duke University Press.

Whitehead, T. 1986. Breakdown, Resolution, and Coherence: The Fieldwork Experiences of a Big, Brown, Pretty-Talking Man in a West Indian Community. In *Self, Sex, and Gender in Cross-cultural Fieldwork*, ed. T. Whitehead and M. Conaway, 213–39. Urbana: University of Illinois Press.

———. 1997. Urban Low-Income African-American Men, HIV/AIDS, and Gender Identity. *Medical Anthropology Quarterly* 11(4):411–47.

Willis, W., Jr. 1971. Divide and Rule: Red, White, and Black in the Southeast. In *Red, White, and Black: Symposium on Indians in the Old South*, ed. C. Hudson, 99–115. Athens: University of Georgia Press.

Wilson, P. 1995 [1973]. *Crab Antics: The Social Anthropology of English-Speaking Societies of the Caribbean*. Prospect Heights: Waveland Press.

Fish and Grits: Southern, African, and British Influences in Bahamian Foodways

Paul Farnsworth and Laurie A. Wilkie

The national cuisine of the Bahamas still very much reflects the diverse ethnic and regional backgrounds of the people of the Loyalist period, drawing upon African, Caribbean, Anglo, and southern American cooking traditions. For visitors accustomed to traveling in other parts of the Caribbean, the melding of U.S. southern colonial cuisine, itself the result of African-European creolization, with African and Caribbean Creole foods is a completely new experience. Whole snappers, first scored and seasoned with homemade pepper sauce, then lightly fried, are identical to those described in contemporary cookbooks of West African food (Hafner 1993; Hultman 1985). Fish, goat (locally referred to as "mutton"), chicken, and beef are chopped into small pieces, bones in place, for their use in souses, as is the practice on Jamaica. The marrow from the bones enriches the broth and enhances the nutritional value of the dish. Conch salad, with its lime- and orange-juice-soaked bell peppers, onions, hot peppers, green tomatoes, and sea salt accompanying luscious chunks of raw conch, suggests ongoing Spanish and Latin American influences. Corn bread, locally known as "Johnny Cake," and the ubiquitousness of local fried chicken establishments speak of southern U.S. influences, while "Guava duff," a steamed dessert pudding, recalls the influences of the British Empire.

Perhaps the dish that best exemplifies the marriage of cultural heritages present in Bahamian food is the one heralded as the "national breakfast" of the Bahamas—corned beef hash and grits. On the surface, this may sound like a simple blend of British and southern influences. Corned beef is indeed part of the hash, used in a very minced form, but so are onions, peppers, and a rich, thick gravy. It would best be described as a "breakfast stew" served with grits. The foodways of the Bahamas are one legacy of a complex social, political, and economic system that intimately tied together the American South, the Caribbean, and Africa during the late eighteenth to the early twentieth centuries. This legacy bears testimony to the creativity and resiliency of a population that has survived the deprivations of colonialism and enslavement.

We were drawn to the Bahamas as an archaeological research area precisely because of its Caribbean—yet not Caribbean—history and culture. The islands of the Bahamas are not in the Caribbean, but in the North Atlantic, stretching from the Greater Antilles to Florida. Caribbean scholars are often quick to point out that the Bahamas are not technically part of the Caribbean. Yet, the colonial Bahamas were economically, socially, and politically as much a part of the British Caribbean as Jamaica or Barbados. However, the Bahamas were also a kind of frontier or borderland of the British Empire, situated in the middle of trade routes of the Spanish colonial empire and the American colonies, and later, the United States. Even the colonial population of the Bahamas owed much to its geographic proximity to the United States and New Spain, for it was not until after the American Revolution that any significant number of people settled in the Bahamas, and the vast majority of these persons were American born.

British Loyalists came in large numbers to the Bahamas between 1783 and 1785, recipients of land grants from a grateful British Crown. Hailing primarily from the Carolinas and Georgia via East Florida, the Loyalists brought with them large numbers of enslaved people. The Loyalist influx radically changed the face of enslavement in the Bahamas (Craton and Saunders 1992). William Wylly indicated in *A Short Account of the Bahamas Islands* that as of 1788 the 330 newly arrived white heads of household had brought with them 3762 enslaved people, who were added to the estimated 1974 "old slaves" already established there. It has been estimated that by 1807 the enslaved population numbered over 11,000—compared to a white population of 3525 and a free colored population of 1485 (Craton and Saunders 1992:180). The 1810 census for the Bahamas indicated a slave population of 11,146 persons (Saunders 1985:48).

The Loyalist planters were not content to depend solely upon the labors of their Creole slaves, and they began importing additional people directly from Africa. During the Loyalist period, at least another nine thousand slaves were brought to these islands (Eltis et al. 1999). How Africans and African Americans who had lived in the American South engaged with this other African population to create the culture of the Bahamas has been the focus of our research in the islands for over a decade. In this paper, we will focus on the Loyalist-period foodways as evidenced from textual and archaeological sources.

While the differing influences on the composition of Bahamian cuisine can be inferred from its modern (and still changing forms), the cultural contacts, fusions, borrowings, and changes that led to the cuisine—the interpersonal and social relationships the food is a by-product of—shapes our archaeological consideration of what we refer to as foodways. By foodways, we are referring to the holistic cultural package that surrounds the procurement, preparation, consumption, and celebration of food (e.g., Mintz 1997; Deetz 1993; Goody 1982; Weismantle 2001). To study foodways is to consider the ways that food is given value and meaning by those who create it and consume it. Foodways are simultaneously one of the most pliable and most conservative of cultural practices. New ingredients and techniques can be quickly incorporated to suit differing access to resources, yet meal structure, preparation, and service can remain remarkably intact.

From 1996 to 2000, we conducted historical archaeological work at Clifton Plantation, a Loyalist plantation located on the Island of New Providence (Figure 1). The plantation was occupied between 1809 and 1828 by the enslaved people of William Wylly. Eight structures associated with the slave village are still standing. We conducted significant excavations in the yards of five of these houses, which are designated as Locus F (a kitchen and residence), Locus G (the slave driver's house), and Loci H, I, and L, which were all additional domestic structures (Figure 2). Based on historical records, the enslaved population of Clifton numbered around fifty to sixty persons who had originated in Africa, the Bahamas, other parts of the Caribbean, and the American South; as such, the community of Clifton can be seen as a community that was demographically typical of the Bahamas in general. On a microscalar level, the Clifton community's engagements with food can be seen as representative of the broader Bahamian experience of the time.

THE ORIGINS OF AFRICANS IN THE BAHAMAS

Africans were not brought to the Bahamas in large numbers prior to the Loyalist period. In 1730 the *Nassau* brought a cargo of 133 people from

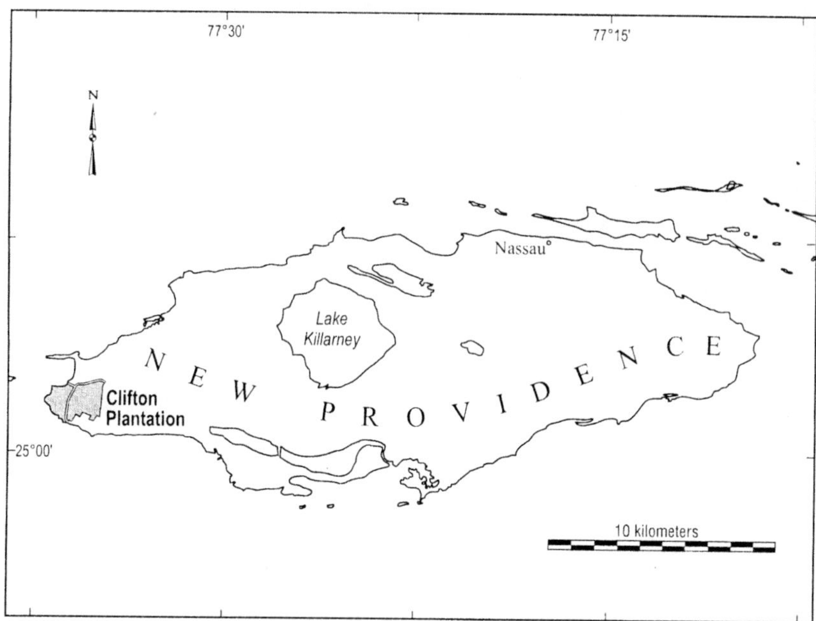

Figure 1. Location of Clifton Plantation on the Island of New Providence, Bahamas.

the Gold Coast; in 1754 another 277 persons were brought from the Gold Coast; and in 1762, 137 people were brought to the Bahamas from an undisclosed location (Eltis et al. 1999). In total, 842 Africans were verifiably brought to the Bahamas prior to the Loyalist period. The Bahamas slave population did not grow quickly at first. In 1731, based on the census, 453 enslaved people (32.6 percent of the population) were recorded living in the Bahamas. There is only a difference of 25 persons between the number documented as being brought to the Bahamas and the 1731 population. This was not to be the case for long. Before the influx of the Loyalists, in 1773, the population of the Bahamas was recorded in a governor's report as totaling 4143 persons, of whom 52.9 percent (around 2192 people) were enslaved (Craton and Saunders 1992:120–21, 162). Writers of the period credited natural reproduction for much of the increase (Craton and Saunders 1992:163).

African Origins of the Creole Slaves

Loyalists brought enslaved people with them from Georgia and the Carolinas via East Florida. One Jamaican planter noted in the 1780s that most

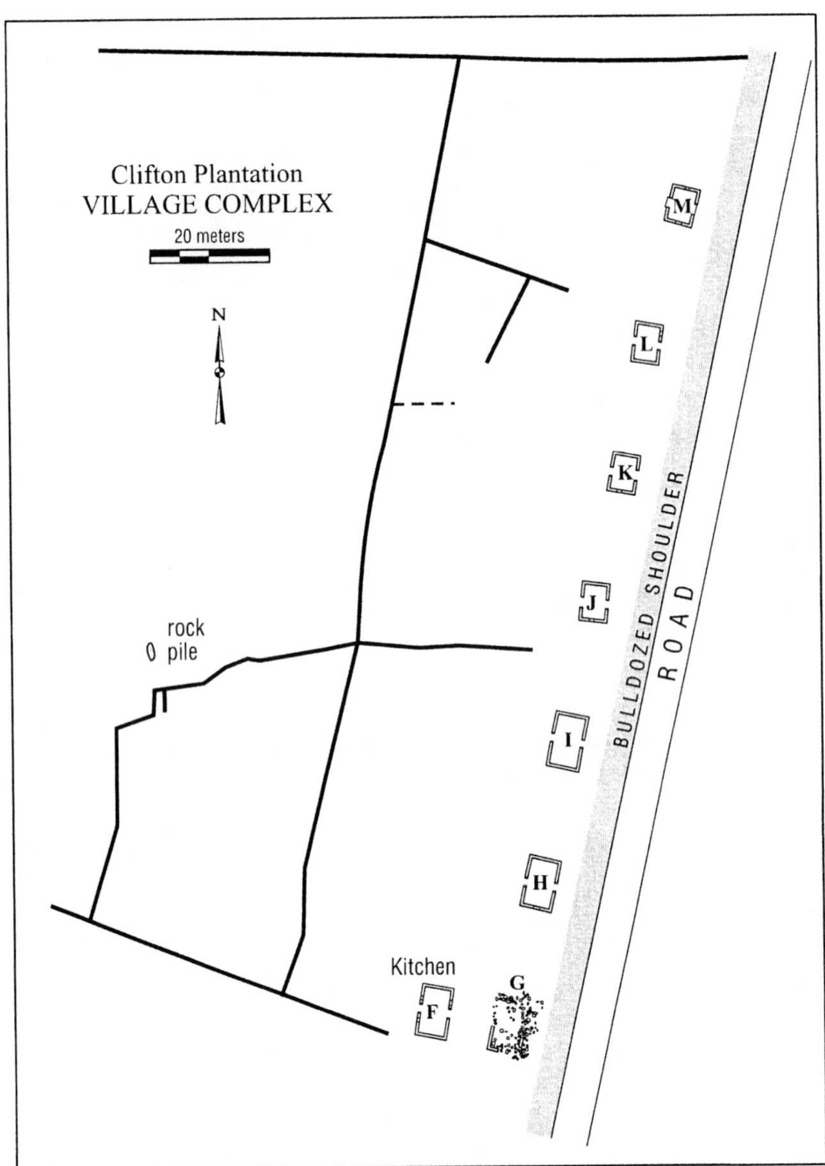

Figure 2. Layout of the slave village at Clifton Plantation.

of the African slaves of the Loyalists were principally Senegambians and Angolans (Mullins 1992:288). Elizabeth Donnan's (1931) work based on cargo lists indicates that nearly 60 percent of the slaves identifiable by origin being brought to Charleston from 1749 to 1787 were Senegambians and peoples from the Windward Coast (the area of modern Liberia and Sierra Leone). Peoples from the Gold Coast and Angola accounted for roughly 15 percent each. Charleston was, of course, the major entry port for most Africans brought to the South during this time, and not all of the persons would have been settled in the Carolinas. The observation that the Loyalist slaves were mainly Senegambians and Angolans aligns with the research of scholars working in the Carolinas from both documentary and archaeological sources (e.g., Creel 1988; Gomez 1996; Ferguson 1992; Joyner 1984; Littlefield 1981). Carolina planters depended upon the rice-cultivating background of the peoples of Sierra Leone and Senegambia to build their agricultural economy (Ferguson 1992; Joyner 1984; Creel 1988).

Senegambia had been an important source of enslaved people early in the trade, supplying 9.7 percent of the British trade from 1700 to 1719. The peak came during 1710 to 1739, when 14.5 percent of the British trade was from this region (Richardson 1989). By the time of the Loyalist period, however, Senegambia was no longer a significant source of enslaved people. This is important to note because the Senegambians brought from the Carolinas and Georgia to the Bahamas would have already spent much of their adult lives away from their motherland. The culture they contributed to the Bahamas would have already been the product of cultural change and adaptation.

In contrast, the areas of Sierra Leone and Central Africa remained important sources of slaves during the Loyalist period (Table 1), and as we will discuss shortly, persons from this area comprised a significant proportion of what we can reconstruct of the Bahamas trade. From 1710 to 1739, nearly a third of all people being seized by the British Trade originated in West Central Africa. From 1700 to 1779, this area provided 21 percent of the British trade. From 1790 to the end of the trade in 1807, West Central Africa was once again an important source of slaves, providing an average of 25 percent of the people (Richardson 1989).

The slaves brought by the Loyalists from the South to the Bahamas were likely to have come from a limited number of African regions: Senegambia, Sierra Leone, and Central Africa. Accompanying the remaining African-born component of the Loyalist slave population would have been their Creole children and grandchildren. While the Americas would have been

Table 1
African Slaves Brought to the Bahamas during the Loyalist Period

Year	*Number of Slave Ships Brought to Bahamas*	*Number of People Brought*	*Identified Geographic Sources (Sources not identified for all ships; other groups could be included.)*
1788	3	726	Windward, Angola
1789	1	72	Windward
1790	0	0	
1791	1	64	Windward
1792	1	210	Sierra Leone
1793	1	216	Sierra Leone
1794	0	0	
1795	1	247	Sierra Leone
1796	0	0	
1797	1	233	
1798	0	91	
1799	3	476	Senegambia, Windward, Gold Coast, Sierra Leone
1800	3	528	Sierra Leone
1801	4	1,066	Sierra Leone
1802	10	2,482	Bight of Biafra, Central Africa
1803	8	2,013	Bight of Biafra, Central Africa
1804	1	638	Sierra Leone, Central Africa, Angola
1805	1	341	Central Africa
1806	1	157	Senegambia
1807	0	0	
Total		*9,560*	

the only world known to these younger generations, that is not to say that they came to the Bahamas without a sense of their African heritage. Leland Ferguson (1992) has demonstrated through his archaeological research that Congo healing arts and aesthetic traditions were well established in South Carolina. Margaret Creel (1988) has convincingly argued that the *poro* and *sande* secret societies, among other elements of Sierra Leone society, informed religious life and community structure in the Sea Islands. The influence of Senegambia and Sierra Leone is clearly seen in the rice-based cuisines that developed in the area (Joyner 1984; Littlefield 1981).

Table 2
The Regional Distribution of British Slave Exports from the West Coast of Africa, 1780–1807

	Number of People Imported	*Percentage of Trade*
Senegambia	5,520	.5%
Sierra Leone	146,920	14.1%
Gold Coast	118,660	11.4%
Bight of Benin	34,840	3.3%
Bight of Biafra	504,070	48.2%
West Central Africa	233,860	22.4%

Compiled from Richardson 1989:Table 5.

The persons brought to the Bahamas via South Carolina had already spent generations engaged in the cultural construction of New World identities.

The African Trade in the Bahamas

The Loyalist period was characterized by a large increase in the slave trade to the Bahamas. During the Loyalist period, the Bahamas became part of an extensive trading network that tied together Liverpool, the West African coast, and the Caribbean. Forty ships were identified that brought 9560 enslaved Africans to the Bahamas between 1788 and 1806, a period of only twenty years (Table 2).

Of the 9560 people brought to the Bahamas, ship manifests and newspaper advertisements allowed the identification of geographic origin for 6277 persons (Table 3). Of these, the majority were designated as from Sierra Leone (20.6 percent), or more generically, the Windward Coast (3.3 percent). One additional ship carried persons from Sierra Leone but had also picked up slaves from the Gold Coast on the same journey. After Sierra Leone, Central Africa was the next largest proportion of the population at 17.8 percent, followed by peoples from the Bight of Biafra at 15.5 percent. Senegambia accounted for only 5.3 percent of the trade. Shipping records provide some insights into more specific origins for Bahamian African slaves. For Senegambians, Goree was identified as a port of embarkment. Persons from Sierra Leone were taken from Rio Nunez and Isles de Los in the area recognized as Sierra Leone proper; a significant number were also taken from Cape Mount in the area of what is now Liberia. Bonny was

Table 3
Geographic Origins of African Slaves Brought to the Bahamas during the Loyalist Period

African Source	*Number of People Landed in Bahamas*	*Percentage Overall*	*Percentage of Population Identified by Region*
Senegambia	413	4.3	6.6
Sierra Leone	1,674	17.5	26.7
Windward Coast	258	2.7	4.1
Gold Coast/Windward	259	2.7	4.1
Bight of Biafra	2,283	23.9	36.4
West/Central Africa	1,390	14.5	22.1
Unspecified	3,283	34.3	—

the point of embarkment for slaves coming from the Bight of Biafra. Persons from Central Africa were brought from Ambriz, Malembu, Malimba, Meimba, Angola, Congo, KiCongo, and MaiCongo (Eltis et al. 1999).

In reviewing newspaper advertisements for newly arrived slave cargos, we were struck by the predominance of people from the "Windward Coast," Cape Mount being the only specifically named port. Although a number of persons were taken from areas that were clearly within the borders of Sierra Leone, they were never designated as such.

When we compare the trade figures for the Bahamas with the broader British trade (Tables 1 and 2), we see that peoples hailing from the Sierra Leone/Windward Coast of Africa were represented in greater numbers in the Bahamas than in the British trade overall. Whereas people from this area accounted for roughly 24 percent of the Bahamas trade during the Loyalist period, they only comprised 14.1 percent of the British trade overall. It is worth considering that this difference reflects the regional preferences of the consumers.

Persons from Sierra Leone and Senegambia had been favored by Carolina slaveholders due to their expertise in rice cultivation. It may be that familiarity with the ways of these people made them desirable to Loyalist planters. Already having large Creole populations derived from this general culture area would have also facilitated the "seasoning" of new African slaves. Theophilis Conneau, himself a notorious slave trader (1976), spoke of the importance of using seasoned Africans and Creoles to welcome new Africans to the plantations to facilitate their transition to the New World.

While their rice agriculture may have made them desirable in the Carolinas, Sierra Leonians had another skill that would have made them desirable in the context of the Bahamas. A number of visitors to the Sierra Leone region comment on the area's salt production and trade (e.g., Saugnier 1792; Corry 1807). Senegambians are similarly skilled in salt production. In his *Voyage to Senegal*, Jean Baptiste Durand (1806:40) wrote, "The Mandingos are particularly industrious in making salt." While Loyalists may have gone to the Bahamas in hopes of developing sugar or cotton agriculture, it was salt raking, particularly in the Turks and Caicos and on the southern Out Islands, that quickly became the most stable economic opportunity (Craton and Saunders 1992).

The prevalence of "Angolans," many of whom (based on their ports of embarkment) were Congolese, may also result from masters engaging in preferences formed while living in the American South (Donnan 1931; Creel 1988). It is important to note that the Igbo, who were shunned in Georgia and the Carolinas due to their reputations as poor workers who were prone to suicide (Gomez 1998), do enter the Bahamas in large numbers, originating from the port of Bonny in 1802 and 1803. The Igbo entered the Bahamas at a time when slaves were not being purchased for the work they could do, but rather for their potential resale value. Perhaps we could interpret this as evidence of a continuing planter bias against the Igbo as laborers?

The Population of Clifton

There are limited documentary records available that specifically list the people who lived at Clifton. Although the plantation was in existence by 1811, our first textual source on the inhabitants was derived from an 1818 court document. Based upon this information, we know that in 1818 at least fifty-six people were living on Clifton. The 1818 documents indicate that at least thirteen married couples lived and farmed on Clifton. At least forty-nine of the people living on Clifton were enslaved by Wylly. Of the people living on Clifton, at least four were African apprentices, Cudjoe, Terracoe, Appia, and Abuka. These men were apprenticed to Wylly in 1811 and perhaps had lived on Clifton the entire period of their indenture. Born between 1789 and 1792, they arrived in the Bahamas as young men on the *Atrivedo*, a slave cargo ship bound for Cuba. They had lived in their homelands long enough to have undergone at least some coming-of-age rituals, and each man bore some marks of his country. Cudjoe bore country marks on his temples and stomach. Terracoe was described as having country marks on his body. Appia's marks were limited to his temples, while Abuka's are described as on his face (Colonial Office Record [CO] 23/63:292–307). While these men were too young to have lived long as adults in Africa, they were certainly old enough to have vivid memories of practices, customs, and traditions.

Within the slave village at Clifton, the young African apprentices would have encountered a number of older African men and women, several with sons their ages. At least nine of the enslaved people living on Clifton in 1818 were African born. Of the thirteen married couples living at Clifton at that time (including apprentices), nine are known to have at least one African-born head of household, two are known to have had two Creole heads of household, and one couple's origins have not been identified. Clearly, within Clifton, there were a sizeable number of households where some memories of Africa and the trauma of the Middle Passage journey were remembered. Importantly, this distribution of Africans throughout the households indicates that while Creoles accounted for the majority of the population, many of the Creoles were first-generation Bahamians on at least one side of their descent. Cudjoe, Appia, Terracoe, and Abuka potentially shared the additional tie of being shipmates.

Children formed a large part of the Clifton population (CO 23/67:147–53; CO 23/67:153–60). At least twenty-two children under the age of eighteen lived on Clifton. Wylly claimed to be responsible for twenty children who were not employed, and based on his records it would appear that sixteen of these children lived on Clifton. Six children are recorded as being employed on the plantation. They worked as shepherds, cowherds, servants, and caretakers of milk cows. Wylly was entitled to the labor of any child over the age of five (Saunders 1998), and at least one child of this age seems to have been employed attending to milk cows and dairy, with the other person in this position at Clifton being a child of eleven. Cowherds were children between the ages of eleven and fifteen or men and women over the age of fifty. Servants were also young, with one on Clifton being eleven. Boys were more likely than girls to be employed at a younger age. Only one girl under the age of eighteen was employed in a set task for Wylly. Children could help in the maintenance of the provisioning grounds as well as hunting or foraging for marine resources to supplement the diet.

Also listed among the occupations for Wylly's enslaved people are "carpenter" and "Mason." There are two of each listed, but the documents do not specify whom these craftspeople are. We might assume that someone bearing the name "Carpenter John" was a carpenter. If so, he lived on Clifton with his wife, Dye. The identities of the other carpenter and the masons are unknown, and there is no way to know whether theirs are among the names that we have been able to compile from existing documents.

By 1821, the enslaved population of Clifton had grown to sixty-seven persons, but this was the peak of the population, for Wylly left the island of New Providence that year, relocating to St. Vincent. The enslaved population was gradually sold away from Clifton and it was completely dissolved by 1828. What other information can be gleaned about the enslaved population and their attempts to create a community at Clifton must be inferred from archaeological data.

Implications for Foodways

The enslaved workforce of the Bahamas may have contained a mix of American-born and African-born laborers, but historical evidence suggests that many of the Creoles and Africans shared similar cultural ancestry. Archaeological evidence from late seventeenth-century South Carolina suggests that enslaved populations of the South maintained a strong sense of ethnic identity despite the constraints of enslavement. For newly enslaved Africans, the Creole population would not have been completely foreign in their attitudes, practices, or perhaps even languages. The Creole population had already adapted to the dietary conditions of enslavement. Rations of maize and salt pork, supplements to the diet of wild game, methods of juggling house gardens with other labor obligations were familiar and routine. European-manufactured serving and cooking wares had been absorbed into techniques of food preparation and service.

Enslaved Africans in the American South encountered their own unique set of food circumstances and responded accordingly. A. L. Tommie Bass (1988:2) described Southern cooking as "meal, meat and molasses." Salt pork served as both main provisioned meat and main protein. Used sparingly so it would last, it was added to many recipes to impart some depth of flavor to dishes. Benne (sesame seed) found its way to South Carolina and was made into a biscuit similar to those now made in the Bahamas. Okra, another African crop, was cultivated and became the basis for stews and gumbos. Corn, or maize, was imported to Africa during the slave trade but in the American South became the staple food for many enslaved people. The creativity displayed by enslaved cooks in regards to this food is beyond compare. Corn bread, corn pancakes, grits, fried hominy, fritters, corn porridges, light soufflélike dishes, and an array of dredges for fried foods were all derived from the simple corn kernel. The Creole population brought to the Bahamas collectively offered one set of solutions to the problem of how to construct foodways during enslavement, and given their cultural heritage, they were likely to have done so along principles and practices familiar to the newly enslaved Africans.

The foods of the New World would not have been foreign to West Africans of the late eighteenth and early nineteenth centuries, either. African agriculture had already been Americanized to a certain extent. Maize, introduced to West Africa by 1500, quickly became widely cultivated (Lewicki and Johnson 1974:20). It is clear from accounts that by the 1800s maize was widespread (e.g., Bosman 1814; Corry 1807; Winterbottom 1803). William Gray, in his 1818 to 1821 accounts of travels through the Niger and Gambia River regions describes maize as an important cultigen. In the capital of Foota Jallon, he described the Foolahs as cultivating "indigo, cotton, rice, maize, yams, cassada [sic] sholots [sic]" among other goods (Gray 1825:37). At Bondoo, he found people to be cultivating "rice, corn in 4 varieties, pumpkins, watermelons gourds, sorrell, onions, tobacco, red pepper, pistachios, cotton and indigo" (Gray 1825:174). Goldberry, traveling through the Bambuk country from 1785 to 1787, described the Mende as raising maize, cassava, sweet potatoes or beans, watermelons, and pistachios (Leiwicki and Johnson 1974:20). Cruickshank (1966:272) describes peoples of the Gold Coast growing corn, yams, cassada, ground-nuts, plantains, and bananas, as well as pineapples, guavas, limes, lemons, oranges, papaws, custard apples, sour-sops, apples, melons, pumpkins, okra, and "many kinds of peppers." The Africans brought to the Bahamas had likely already incorporated indigenous American plants into their diets. In the Bahamas, these two Americanized African diets—one originating from the American South and one originating in Africa, met and engaged in the Caribbean. Together, these two foodways traditions encountered the unique land and sea resources of the Bahamas.

EVIDENCE OF FOOD REMAINS AT CLIFTON

Food remains, consisting of shellfish remains and animal bone, were recovered from each of the excavation areas. In addition to the actual remains of food, we have a wide range of other materials available to us regarding foodways at Clifton. Documentary evidence, ceramic tablewares and storage vessels, cooking pots, beverage bottles, cutlery, and the use of space all speak to us of the ways that food was experienced at Clifton.

In the Bahamas, planters were required to provision their enslaved people with legally set minimum quantities of corn. Adults were to receive eight quarts of corn and children were given half that amount. Struggling to keep plantations economically viable, Bahamian planters increasingly turned to practices requiring enslaved people to self-provision in return for reduced work loads, land allocations, and additional days of the week off. Wylly also turned to this practice, as described in a November 1, 1817, letter to James Rutherford:

> I see I have done wrong in allowing any corn to the working people, who have Saturday to themselves: It is only an encouragement to idleness: For there are many of them who never will work for themselves, while they continue to receive even their half allowance of corn. To put an end to this waste of time, I now take away that corn; and instead of it, give them Friday, as well as Saturday: but they must work or starve. But should any of them occasionally want provisions, they may have corn out of my Barn, at the rate of four shillings a peck to be paid for in labour. Each man and his wife must plant two acres of Provisions: (which the woman alone will be able to attend): and when they have potatoes or other bulky articles to carry to market, they may use my Boat. (CO 23/67:150)

Among the textual sources associated with Clifton is an accounting of how many acres of land were under cultivation by families living on Clifton and what crops were being cultivated (CO 23/67:164–65). For Clifton, eighteen parcels of land are described as being assigned to families or individuals. The records do not go as far as to document, or even estimate, the amount of each crop produced, but at least we have some indication of what vegetable stuffs were incorporated into the diet. Thirteen of the provisioning grounds at Clifton were described as being cultivated by a man, his wife, and in two cases, also by older children. The remaining five parcels were being cultivated by individuals, two of whom were women, three of whom were men. All of the provisioning grounds were recorded as being in "Good order"; none were described as in "Bad order."

The land parcels are described as the "number of tasks" assigned to each family. The task is a remnant of southern plantation agricultural practice. The term "task" in the Bahamas was used to denote quarter-acre parcels of land, often marked by stones or posts (CO 23/63:16). Intriguingly, there is some evidence to suggest that the task system still shapes some Bahamian farming. In studying agricultural practices on Cat Island during the 1970s, Jane Finkelstein reported the following custom: "A field is sometimes divided into a 'tas.' One tas is equivalent to an area of 50 feet by 100 feet. Upright sticks which are shoved one quarter of the way into the ground, or standing gamalame trees, are used to mark the boundaries of the field" (Finkelstein 1978:77). Finkelstein is clearly describing the task system used in plantation settings during the Loyalist period but apparently did not recognize the term.

At Clifton, provisioning grounds ranged from .5 acres to 4.0 acres, with the average allotment being 2.4 acres. In comparison, at Montpelier plantation in Jamaica, Higman (1998) found that the average slave worker was granted .75 to 1.3 acres. Given that each provisioning ground at Clifton was granted to two to four people, Wylly was not being unusually generous compared to other planters. In total, about 43.3 acres of land at Clifton was being cultivated by the enslaved and apprenticed Africans for their own use. On these grounds, families were reported to be cultivating Indian and Guinea corn (maize and sorghum), yams, potatoes, pumpkins and squashes, peas, beans and ocre (okra), benne (sesame), ground nut (peanuts), eddies (taro), plantains/banana, watermelon, and musk melon.

These crops would have provided greater nutritional benefits than a straight corn ration, with beans, peanuts, and sesame providing important protein and fat sources to the diet if sources of animal protein were scarce. In the crops of Clifton, we can also see African and American dietary influences. Yams, sorghum, and different varieties of beans were traditionally known and cultivated in West Africa, and by the late seventeenth century, the American crops peanuts and plantains were being cultivated in Ghana (DeCorse 2001:112).

Zooarchaeological remains provide us with insights into meat use in the diet (Table 4). Based on the archaeological record at Clifton, land animals accounted for very little of the faunal assemblage. At the kitchen, terrestrial species accounted for only 3.4 percent of the identifiable specimens. Fowl, raccoon, sheep/goat, and a mouse or rat were the only species identified. Raccoon and sheep/goat were most represented with ten specimens each. In contrast, mammals accounted for 26.5 percent of the identified specimens at Locus H. In addition to bird, mouse/rat, raccoon, and sheep/goat, there also were pig, cow, and dog. Raccoon was the most abundant of the land animals, accounting for thirty-five of the ninety-one identified specimens; sheep/goat followed with twenty-five identified specimens.

Raccoons are an introduced species found only on New Providence. The animal was established in the Bahamas as early as the 1780s. Schoepf, a visitor during this time wrote, "The Racoon is found only on Providence island,

Table 4
Identified Animal Remains Recovered from Clifton's Village

	Locus F		*Locus G*		*Locus H*		*Locus I*		*Locus L*	
Species	*MNI*	*NISP*	*MNI*	*NISP*	*MNI*	*NISP*	*MNI*	*NISP*	*MNI*	*NISP*
Canis familiaris					1	1				
Procyon lotor	1	10	1	4	2	38			1	3
Sus scrofa			1	1	1	5			1	2
Bos taurus					1	8			1	3
Caprinae	1	10	1	4	1	25	1	3		
Murinae	1	3			2	11			1	2
Class Aves	1	2	1	3	1	2				
Gallus gallus							2	2		
Pomacanthidae			1	2						
Serranidae	16	230	2	26	13	97	1	3	1	10
Carangidae	2	13			1	2				
Belonidae	1	1								
Haemulidae	23	195	1	20	5	70				
Lutjanidae	11	162	2	29	5	35	2	2		
Sparidae	7	41	2	7	3	28				
Sphyraenidae	1	6			1	2			1	1
Scaridae	6	19	1	4	2	7			1	1
Labridae	4	24	1	2	1	5				
Holocentridae			1	3						
Balistidae	1	5			1	1			1	1
Total		*721*		*107*		*337*		*10*		*23*

of which it is no more originally native than the rats and mice brought in by ships. From one or more tame pairs of these droll beasts, brought over by the curious from the main-land, and afterwards escaped by chance into the woods, the race has amazingly increased, to the great vexation and damage of the inhabitants, who can scarcely protect their house-fowls from these stealthy thieves" (Schoepf 1911:289). Schoepf spends a great deal of time elsewhere in his account describing the exotic food habits of the islands, such as the consumption of chiton, iguanas and marmot. In this context, it is surprising that he does not mention the consumption of raccoon, particularly since it was seen as a pest. Miller, in a 1905 study of Bahamian mammals, wrote of the raccoon, "there is a tradition that this animal had been introduced by one of the large plantation owners, many, many years ago, but from where there seemed to be complete uncertainty. I was told Florida, but this seemed to be only a conjecture." Today, raccoon is consumed on New Providence, though its consumption seems to have some negative connotations.

By the time of Clifton's occupation, raccoon was clearly being consumed. Several of the raccoon bones showed unmistakable signs of butchering. This animal was present in four of the five slave village faunal assemblages, demonstrating that this resource was widely utilized by the community. Given the North American origin of this species, its incorporation in the diet at Clifton probably reflects the influences of the people who had been raised in the American South. Zooarchaeological analyses of plantation diet in the American South have demonstrated that raccoon was an important wild food resource used to supplement meager provisions (Franklin 1997; Reitz 1994). The preparation of the meat was not straightforward, however. Raccoons contain a number of musk glands that are concentrated on their lower back and haunches. If these glands are pricked during skinning or preparation, they impart a foul scent and flavor to the meat. It is likely that one of Clifton's southern-born Creoles provided the knowledge that enabled the villagers to use raccoon meat. The consumption of raccoon had an additional potential social value for the people of Clifton that is worth briefly considering. Many West African societies recognize food taboos that are related to lineages or religious practice (Lewicki and Johnson 1974). The diverse community of Clifton was likely to have included a range of food restrictions among its members, be they Muslim or honoring other traditions. Unlike goats, pigs, sheep, cows, fish, chickens, and dogs, raccoons had no equivalent in Africa and may have been a "safe" food resource for at least the non-Muslim component of the population.

The minimal consumption of domesticated animals in the diet at Clifton is at first surprising when one realizes that in 1818, of the people allocated provisioning grounds on Clifton, all but one family is recorded as raising fowl, and ten of the eighteen are noted as raising hogs. However, in his answers to 1815 African Institute questions, Wylly describes provisioning practices in the Bahamas: "They are allowed as much ground as they choose to cultivate, and are universally permitted to raise Hogs and Poultry. Yet it is true to a Proverb that 'No negroe ever eats his own Fowl or kills his own Pig. They sell them all'" (CO 23/63:16).

As we have discussed elsewhere (e.g., Wilkie and Farnsworth 1999; Wilkie 2001), the household goods recovered from the slave village at Clifton are extremely diverse and include many items that would be seen as communicating wealth. The quality of goods recovered from Clifton is particularly striking when compared to goods recovered from other enslaved house sites in the Bahamas (Farnsworth 1996). Clearly, in looking at foodways at Clifton, we must consider how the composition of the diet was shaped by the community's desire to participate fully in the consumer culture of Nassau.

Perhaps given this competing economic agenda, it is not surprising that locally procured shellfish and bony fish provided the vast bulk of meat brought to and consumed at Clifton. One would not need to venture far to obtain these resources, merely to the shore's edge about six hundred meters away, where they could be collected from the reef system of Clifton Bay. Bahamians eat a wide range of fish species, but some are preferred over others. Oral histories and documentary evidence provide some insights into which species were favored. In his collection of oral histories from Bain Town, one of the historic subdivisions of Nassau's African section, Eneas provides insights into fish preferences and preparation. He estimated that his oral history provided a glimpse into Bain Town's past from at least the 1890s through 1970. Eneas (1976:59) wrote: "There was a large variety of fish: we had snappers, margaret fish, turbots, grunts, hinds, porgies and grouper, to name a few. Many of these were forbidden by my mother, who had her preferences when it came down to the manner in which she wanted to prepare them. Only grunts, snappers, Jacks, goggle eyes and smaller Margaret fish were fried in our house." Eneas also remembered grouper being boiled and served over corn grits to make a filling meal. Today, boiled grouper with corn bread or grits is considered a special Sunday breakfast.

A 1903 visitor to the Bahamas wrote, "The following kinds are *esteemed* as food: snapper, mutton fish, groupers, pompano, grunts, jacks, runners, porgies, angelfish, porkfish, hogfish, tangs, turbots and shellfish. Those considered of *fair quality* are: bonito, kingfish, shad, goat fish, mullet, goggle eyes, squirrel fish, houndfish, flying fish, amber fish or amber jack, etc." (Bean 1905:294, emphasis added). Note that almost exclusively the fish described as "esteemed" are those species that are easily acquired over reefs close to shore and tend toward ten inches or greater in length. Less favored species are those that are smaller or that can only be acquired further from the reefs. Off the Southeast American and West African coasts, species such as tuna, snappers, jack, shad, and mullet could be acquired given access to a boat. Most species recovered from southern sites, however, are freshwater fish like catfish, crappie, bluegills, gar, and other panfish (e.g., Franklin 2001; Mullins 1999; Reitz 1994). Freshwater sources were also important in Africa. No freshwater fish are found in the Bahamas.

Fish bone was recovered from Loci F, G, H, I, and L, though in greatly varying amounts. A comparison of the fish bone reveals that the greatest number of identified elements came from seabasses, grunts, snappers, and porgies. These families accounted for 90 percent of the specimens identified from the kitchen, 93 percent of the specimens identified from the houseyard at H, and 86 percent at Locus G. The prevalence of less-abundant fish varies slightly, with a greater percentage of wrasses identified at the kitchen and a slightly greater percentage of parrot fishes being recovered from the houseyards at G and H.

While the composition of the faunal assemblage demonstrated that the same fish were deposited in about the same proportion, there were differences in what parts of the fish were represented. At four of the house sites, grouper assemblages were predominantly composed of head elements, whereas smaller fish like grunts, snappers, and hinds were represented by bones from the entire body. This would suggest that enslaved people were using pan fish similar to those used today, as well as taking advantage of the planter's disinterest in grouper heads.

Shellfish were recovered from each of the house sites, though with varying densities. A total of 2,469 pieces of shell, representing a minimum of 206 individuals from 40 species were found at the H house yard, and 1,034 fragments, representing a minimum of 200 individuals from 26 species, were found at the kitchen. When we compare the amount of flesh represented by a particular species, the same four shellfish species accounted for the vast majority of the protein at each locus (Table 5), with queen conch (*Strombus gigas*) the most important followed by tiger lucine (*Codakia*

Table 5
Most Abundant Shell Species Recovered from the Village

	Locus F		*Locus G*		*Locus H*		*Locus I*		*Locus L*	
Species	*NISP*	*MNI*	*NISP*	*MNI*	*NISP*	*MNI*	*NISP*	*MNI*	*NISP*	*MNI*
Acanthopleura granulate (Fuzzy Chiton)	162	26	69	10	435	49	44	6	27	8
Cittarium pica (West Indian Top Shell)	330	30	608	47	519	21	361	12	294	20
Strombus gigas (Queen Conch)	231	24	457	70	487	9	102	6	56	10
Codakia orbicularis (Tiger Lucine)	148	61	221	58	598	55	460	40	120	26
Tellina radiata (Sunrise Tellin)	16	6	7	2	109	12	66	4	8	2

orbicularis), welk/west indian top shell (*Cittarium pica*), and curbs/chiton (*Acantholeria granulata* and *Chiton tuberculatus*).

The consumption of shellfish had some negative connotations early in the Loyalist period. Schoepf (1911:295) wrote in 1793: "Conchs and welks are eaten by the less fastidious of the inhabitants, as are a variety of the lepas (chiton) which everywhere clings fast to the rocks by the sea." Yet one Loyalist guest in the early 1800s described eating chiton while on an outing. "On the edges of the rock near the water we knocked off several curbs as they are called. They are I believe of the Chiton genus of shells and cling to the rock on their under surface with great tenacity. The flesh is like the periwinkle and conch but pleasanter and is preferred raw" (Fries 1968:32). Perhaps the oysters and other shellfish of the eastern seaboard left the Loyalists more open to the consumption of shellfish than the white Bahamian settlers who preceded them.

Fish and shellfish were clearly the most important meat resources within the village, despite the almost universal raising of fowl and, in many cases, hogs. The emphasis on the consumption of marine resources represents both a cultural continuity in coastal West African foodways and an economic strategy commonly employed in the American South, where fish and shellfish often were used to supplement meager rations.

Food in the Clifton village would have been a collective endeavor, building on the contributions of knowledge and experience from various families as they were exposed to one another's traditions, either through the sharing of food in the yard or through redistribution of food through the kitchen. The creation of a common cuisine would have been facilitated by the familiarity with African and New World crops that is likely to have been shared by all members of the village. Yet we might also expect that meals maintained an idiosyncratic aspect to them, with particular foods or taboos, seasoning, and consumption traditions being particular to individual families.

FOOD PREPARATION AND CONSUMPTION

The zooarchaeological evidence suggests that one-pot cooking probably accounts for much of the food preparation in the village; fish heads, most of the shellfish, and raccoon are most easily prepared in this manner. Smaller "pan" fish were probably fried and consumed off the bone. The highly fragmented nature of the domestic animal bones mimics patterns seen in the ethnographic and archaeological records of Ghana and Jamaica, where marrow is extracted from long bones—a practice also seen in the Bahamas.

We can derive some generalizations about past dietary practices based on travel accounts. Lewicki and Johnson (1974:79) advise: "By comparison with food of vegetable origin, meat played only a minor part in the nourishment of West African peoples during the middle ages. It is probable that many tribes ate meat only to celebrate some religious rite or on some equally solemn occasion." Cruickshank (1966:275) makes a similar observation for the peoples of the Gold Coast: "They do not make use of much animal food, not that they do not care for it, but because it is not abundant." Cruickshank further stated that dried fish was one of the chief relishes used in the Gold Coast region (modern Ghana). This is a sentiment mirrored by two authors of contemporary African cooking, one of whom observes that meat is used more as a seasoning than as a main focus of a dish (Hafner 1993). The rations of slavery diet, which provided little in the way of meat, would have reinforced this tradition.

In contrast, Gray (1825:266) describes the people of the Kingdom of Galam as being "proverbially fond of animal food, which, although arrived at a higher degree of keeping than would please the palates of our most decided epicures, would not be rejected by them." Gray later describes having "an excellent supper of rice and mutton" at Kirrijou, where people raised "corn, rice, ground-nuts and onions" (Gray 1825:299–300), perhaps providing some insight into ingredients that may have also been used in the dish. Perhaps as a legacy of the impoverished rations of the past, Bahamians today see meat as an important element of any meal.

The most common historically recorded dishes in West Africa using grains and yams were porridges (Lewicki and Johnson 1974; Gray 1825; Cruickshank 1853). In the nineteenth century, Reisen Barth reported eating a porridge of sorghum that was covered with meat and soup (a stew?) (Lewicki and Johnson 1974:45). "Fufu", made of pounded yam, cassava, or plantain, is a staple starch dish in Ghana (DeCorse 2001:104). Yams and other tubers were likewise boiled and mashed into a porridge among the Ashanti (Rattray 1979:51, 52). Rattray describes fufu as pounded yams or plantain, distinguishing it from eto, which is mashed yams. Cruickshank's earlier observations in the area provide similar detail. "They live principally upon bread made from the Indian corn, and upon yams and plantains, which they mash, or cut up into pieces, making a vegetable soup, which is highly seasoned with peppers" (Cruickshank 1853:274).

Fufu, according to Rattray, is pounded in a rough wooden mortar called a *dasie* (1979:235). We found a mortar being used by an elderly woman on Crooked Island that is identical to mortars found in West Africa. The mortar is essentially a hollow scooped out of a tree trunk. A long limb is used as a pestle, raised over the head and dropped repeatedly into the mortar. The weight and the velocity of the dropping pestle provide the crushing power of the instrument. In northern Nigeria, benne, or sesame seeds, were also reportedly made into porridge as well as utilized for their oil (Lewicki and Johnson 1974:110).

Winterbottom (1803:64–65) assessed Gold Coast and Sierra Leone diets in a similar way. "The diet of the Africans is simple and consists chiefly of boiled rice and palm oil, to which is occasionally added a small proportion of animal food. Their art of cookery is confined to boiling or stewing . . . the natives on the Gold Coast are remarkable for seasoning their food very high with capsicum, in what they call black soup." In Sierra Leone, he recorded that they used bird pepper (*Capsicum frutescens*) to flavor their food.

Starchy porridges are also to be found in the American South. Corn meal is boiled with water or milk to make a thick porridge, sometimes referred to as couche-couche (Wilkie 2000), and grits is likewise hominy porridge. While rice is now the most common accompaniment to meals both in the

Bahamas and the American South, porridges were still known in the Bahamas in the early twentieth century. Eneas (1976:60) recalled "old Yorubas" in Bain Town using cornmeal to make "foo foo," which was covered with an okra soup.

Writing of the late nineteenth and early twentieth century, Eneas recalled several old Bahamian dishes that elders attributed to an African origin. "A'ncara," which was "a vegetable meat ball . . . they were made from legumes, okras, onions, pepper, and a mix; this was fried in the form of balls" (Eneas 1976:62). In the Niger region, Arabic explorers encountered Fulani and Songhai speakers making "onion balls" that were made of butter and a dried, ground, onion mixture (Johnson and Lewicki 1974:59). "Agidi" was a desert wrapped in almond leaves and served with milk and sugar. "Mi, Mi" was also wrapped in leaves and was highly spiced and made from maize (Eneas 1976:62).

Although Eneas (1976) has specifically attributed these foods to continuities in the Yoruba diet, in reality, these are dishes found throughout West Africa. For instance, Hafner (1993:41) describes "Akara" as fried bean balls common in West Africa and especially popular among Muslims. She has found them prepared as well in Jamaica and Trinidad. Versions of okra stew and soup are likewise found throughout West Africa. Adaptations of these dishes can also be found in the American South. FuFu, Kenkey, and Banku, are all variations on a similar type of dish—a starch the consistency of mashed potatoes or thicker—that is served accompanied by a soup or stew. Kenkey is made by the coastal Fanti from soaked and partially fermented corn (DeCorse 2001:104), and Banku, a cornmeal dumpling, is commonly found among the Congolese. In the American South, fritters and hushpuppies are reminiscent of this food as well. Hutchinson (1858:39) described women in Sierra Leone selling "Agiddy" on the streets, describing it as "the Papaw title for Indian corn bruised with water into a gruel-like presentation." Agiddy sounds remarkably like couche-couche or grits from the American South.

The provisioning grounds of Clifton also provided the opportunity to prepare African-style beverages. The eighteenth century traveler Golbéry, exploring between 1785 and 1787, described the people of Bambuk (in western Mali) producing a millet-based alcoholic drink. Millet was placed in an earthen pot filled with water and kept until it turned sour. Honey was then added to the pot, and it was left in the sun for ten days. The drink was filtered, producing a strong, meadlike beverage (Lewicki and Johnson 1974:129). Beer brewing in Senegambia (also western Mali) at the end of the eighteenth century (1795–1797) was described by the explorer Mungo Park (Park 2000). The nineteenth century explorer Caillié noted that specialist brewers of beer existed among the Bambara who traveled to festivals and sold beer in small calabashes (Lewicki and Johnson 1974:225).

Women typically brew beer in West Africa (e.g., Berns 1988; Forde 1951; Meek 1931, 1950; Rattray 1932), although depending upon its purpose there may be strict taboos that hinder production or restrict participation. For example, Jukun women may not taste the beer at any point if it is being brewed for religious purposes, and menstruating women cannot prepare beer for use by the king or in any religious ceremony (Meek 1950:145, 442).

While the temperatures in the Bahamas would have been viewed as generally too hot for brewing by British brewers of the time (Sambrook 1996:154–65), they are little different from those of West Africa. The raw materials for African-style beer were not in short supply either, for plantations in the Bahamas grew and issued maize and guinea corn (sorghum) to their slaves. Further, most enslaved people grew these grains in their own provision grounds as well (CO 23.67:103–12). On Clifton, enslaved families are documented as growing sorghum and maize in their gardens, in addition to receiving maize rations. All that was required to make beer was a large vessel for boiling beer and other containers for fermenting it.

Beer was not the only alcoholic beverage created by Africans. Palm wine was probably one of the more famous food products of the Gold Coast. Cruickshank (1966:275) writes of this beverage: "They make a very pleasant and palatable wine from the palm species of trees. This is done by uprooting the tree, lopping off its leaves, and perforating the trunk. They place a calabash at the puncture, and burn some dried twigs under the tree. The sap is thus forced to the orifice, and received into the pot, into which it distils for several days . . . the wine is fresh and very pleasant to drink when new; but if allowed to stand for some hours it ferments rapidly, and becomes pungent and intoxicating."

The brewing of alcoholic beverages was also practiced in the American South, where corn whiskey, persimmon wine, and honey locust wine are all described in the ex-slave narratives. Genovese (1976:644) notes that persimmon or locust beer or cider were consumed at dances and that they were home brewed without objection from the planter. William B. Smith of Virginia, writing in 1838, described a house servant who never failed to invite him in to sample his persimmon beer whenever he passed his house (Genovese 1974:644). A former slave in Louisiana described brewing persimmon beer (Saxon and Tallant 1987:239). The first steps in making "moonshine" whiskey are the same as making African beers (the fermentation of grain/maize). In her 1997 dissertation describing archaeological research at a slave cabin at Rich Neck Plantation, Virginia, Maria Franklin (1997:211–12) reports that persimmons and honey locust pods were among the most abundant floral remains from the site. She notes that both of these plants were used to make fermented beverages described in ex-slave narratives. We must consider not only that the people of Clifton purchased alcoholic beverages, but also that they had the ingredients and means of producing their own alcohol.

While the religious connotations and ritual associations for particular foods and beverages may have varied greatly from one African ethnic group to another, the reality is that the ingredients and materiality of food and beverage preparation were commonly held across many ethnic boundaries. As a result of these shared experiences and expectations regarding foods, food preparation and, as we will soon see, consumption, was a routine and familiar arena in which families from multiple cultural and regional backgrounds could forge commonalities with one another.

Food preparation artifacts recovered from the village and beach houses on Clifton were limited to cast-iron pots that were set up on three or four feet. Deceptively simple, these pots can be used for a variety of cooking techniques. Covered, a pot can be used to roast meats, to bake simple breads and biscuits, or to steam foods. Uncovered, pots can be used to boil liquids, simmer stews, or fry and sauté foods. The limitations are not in the vessel, only the imagination. With access to a cast-iron pot, most of the African and Bahamian dishes we have described can be prepared. There is no evidence that the families of Clifton used any other cooking vessel of consequence.

Stoneware crocks of varying sizes and shapes were also recovered from every household. Unlike the cooking pots, which have a clear function, it is not clear how crocks were used; probably they were used for food or beverage storage or for fermenting or pickling food. Cooking is the one activity for which crocks do not seem to have been used—we have recovered no examples of crocks bearing evidence of charring or heating, leading us to conclude that these objects were not used in heating foods. There is a range of other possible uses for these vessels. As noted above, making fermented beverages often required ceramic storage vessels, thus suggesting one possible use. Lewicki and Johnson (1974:58, 101) report that pickling and brining/salting were the most common methods used in West Africa to preserve onions and fish. Crocks could have been used for these.

Crocks also could have been used to store dairy products at Clifton. Milk was a common food product in West Africa. Gray (1825:79) reported that peoples like the Foolahs traded dairy products such as milk and butter for cloth. In the American South, Bass (1988:22) recalled that stoneware jugs were used to sour milk. The clabber could then be removed and drained to make cheese, and the product left behind was buttermilk. With no means of refrigeration, this was the best way to use milk. Lewicki and Johnson (1974) likewise report that West African peoples made cheese through a similar process.

It is also possible that these vessels were used to store dry foods such as corn meal, rice, or other grains. Among the Bachama of Nigeria, Meek (1931:23) described pots being sunk in the ground near grinding stones to easily catch flour. Bura women were reported to keep bins for storing seed in their grinding hut (Meek 1931:143). Yoruba women are reported to favor making ground pepper sauces (Ojo 1966), which would also require storage. Any number of goods produced in the gardens, or even the weekly corn rations, would have required storage to protect the food from insects and rodents.

Bahamian kitchens typically consisted of at least a hearth where a pot could be set in the yard, but they may have had a more elaborate cooking platform and even an oven for baking. In the Bahamian villages of Gambier and Adelaide, women described hearths made of "three stones" to rest a pot on (Anderson 1998). This arrangement mimics closely in design a Ghanaian clay hearth pictured in an 1873 British journal (DeCorse 2001:178). During the excavation of the Locus H yard, we found the base of a limestone platform that was clearly associated with food preparation. The base of this oven is similar to that of a wonderful example of a Bahamian limestone oven pictured on an early twentieth-century Bahamian postcard (Malone and Roberts 1991:57). The oven has a stone base and an enclosed baking arch (Figure 3). In the tropical environment of the Bahamas, houses did not require interior hearths, so much cooking took place in the yard. Although cooking outdoors may have been seasonally practiced in the American South, most slave houses were built with chimneys and internal hearths, where food was also prepared. The use of pottery and iron cooking vessels was, however, the same.

We can see that the Bahamian means of preparing food were simple yet elegant. In contrast, the food-serving materials recovered from Clifton —mainly British ceramics—demonstrate a dazzling variety in decoration (Figure 4). How were these items used in the service and consumption of

Figure 3. Illustration of a Bahamian hearth, based on an historic postcard.

food? Though it is dangerous to generalize the foodways of a culture area as large and diverse as West Africa (Posnansky 1999), we can at least say that the cuisine was characterized by one-pot meals and that communally served starches formed the centerpiece of the meal. People dined together, often seated on mats or stools in the yard or compound area. Bowls were the most commonly used vessel, and food was consumed with spoons or directly from the fingers (DeCorse 2001; Ferguson 1992). Eneas (1976) remembered that while the elder Africans of Bain Town consumed their foods from bowls with their fingers, the children were not allowed to imitate them, but rather were taught to use cutlery. In West Africa, by the seventeenth century, while indigenously made pots were often used in households, at least at El Mina, DeCorse (2001) found that European and Asian ceramics were known and used by elite African families. In addition to pottery, calabashes (gourds) were also modified to make bowls and water storage vessels in West Africa (Price and Price 1980; Agorsah 1994). In 1826 in Jamaica, Barclay observed: "The calabash tree produces a large fruit, not eatable, but nevertheless valuable, as the skin of it is a hard and solid substance, like the shell of a nut, and when scooped out, answers the purpose of holding water, or cut across the middle, makes two cups or dishes. Every negro has his calabash, and may have them carved with figures like those which are tattooed on the skins of the Africans" (Abrahams and Szwed 1983:347). In addition to the ceramics recovered from the site, we must consider the possibility that perishable items, such as "squash" or coconut shells, could have been used for food consumption and storage as well.

Figure 4. Examples of British-manufactured, decorated tablewares found in the slave village of Clifton.

Long-standing African pottery traditions have been noted in many parts of the American South and the Caribbean (such as Jamaica, the Lesser Antilles, and Puerto Rico) (Armstrong 1990; Ferguson 1992; Hauser and Armstrong 1999; Heath 1999; Petersen et al. 1999), but there is no equivalent tradition in the Bahamas. This is not surprising, because even the Lucayan Amerindians, who had little choice about whether or not to produce pottery, found making serviceable vessels from the poor local clay problematic (Keegan 1997). Instead, the people of Clifton relied upon mass-produced European ceramics.

Plate-to-bowl ratios have been commonly employed by archaeologists to determine whether a diet was more dependent upon liquid-based meals or roasted cuts of meat. Working in Jamaica, Armstrong (1990) found at

Drax Hall that when yabba wares and European-manufactured vessels were considered collectively, bowls outnumbered plates recovered from the site. Armstrong attributed this occurrence to continuities in West African dining practices that favor the consumption of liquid-based foods in bowls. A similar kind of pattern could be seen at Montpelier, Jamaica (Higman 1998:222).

At Clifton, if we consider the overall composition of village ceramic assemblages by vessel, we see that plates, bowls, tea wares, and beverage-storage-related artifacts are the most numerously represented (Table 6). No sugar boxes or creamers were recovered from the village, but in addition to many saucers and teacups, typically at least one teapot was recovered from each house site. The driver's house even included an elegant example manufactured of black, dry-bodied stoneware, often referred to as "black basalt." Teapot lids, though not necessarily matching the teapots, were also found at most loci.

It is tempting to wonder how the European vessels might have been used within the village—were they used as they would have been by Europeans, or were they reinterpreted according to different culinary needs and traditions? In a review of British colonial and Anglo-American period cookbooks, Elizabeth Scott (1997) has demonstrated that ceramics were used in a variety of ways in the kitchen for measuring and preparing food. There is no reason to think that the people of Clifton did not make similar innovations. A handled teacup, for instance, would make an excellent water scoop. Similarly, a teacup would be a useful measure for dry goods such as corn meal. Teacups and saucers could equally stand in as small and shallow bowls when dining. In Jamaica, hot broths like fish tea can be consumed from cups. Likewise, in some Bahamian food stands conch chowder is served in a cup and consumed by drinking. Bush medicine, still commonly employed in the Bahamas, is consumed often as a hot tea. Notably, teapots were more abundantly found in the Clifton village than pitchers. Teapots have the advantage of being lidded, therefore providing some protection for the vessel's contents from small flies and bugs that might be attracted to it. Teapots also allow the user to easily disguise contents from others.

Very little evidence of cutlery was recovered from the village and beach area. Unfortunately, in most instances, only the handle was recovered, thus limiting our identification. A single iron spoon and an iron handle were recovered from Locus H; one iron spoon was found at G and L respectively; two iron spoons, a pewter fork, a pewter handle, and an iron knife were found at N; and a pewter handle and an iron spoon were found at P. The

Table 6

Distribution of Ceramics from Clifton Slave Village by Vessel Form

	Locus F		*Locus G*		*Locus H*		*Locus I*		*Locus L*		*Locus N*		*Locus P*	
Vessel Form	#	%	#	%	#	%	#	%	#	%	#	%	#	%
Plate	9	18.3	18	28.6	17	26.6	17	26.6	10	27.7	16	43.2	4	30.8
Bowl	14	28.6	15	23.8	15	23.4	16	25.0	9	25.0	6	16.2	2	15.4
Teawares	19	38.8	20	31.7	24	37.5	20	31.1	7	19.4	7	18.9	4	30.8
Service Vessels	1	2.0	3	4.8	1	1.6	0	0	2	5.6	5	13.5	1	7.5
Beverage Storage	3	6.1	2	3.2	2	3.1	4	6.3	3	8.3	1	2.7		
Food Storage	0	0	0	0	0	0	0	0	0				1	7.5
Food Preparation	1	2.0	3	4.8	2	3.1	7	10.9	3	8.3	1	2.7	1	7.5
Ink wells	1	2.0	2	3.2	1	1.6	0	0	1	2.8				
Sanitation	0	0	0	0	1	1.6			1	2.8	1	2.7		
Figurines	1	2.0	0	0	1	1.6	0	0	0	0				
Total	*49*		*63*		*64*		*64*		*36*		*37*		*13*	

higher incidence of these objects at the beach houses may be the result of more people being housed in these locations. Spoons were the most commonly identified cutlery piece. Spoons would have been used to serve from pots and potentially to mix foods during preparation, as well as for food consumption. Perhaps the families ate as Eneas (1976) remembered the older Yoruba people of Bain Town—with their fingers.

LAYERS OF MEANING AND FOOD

No discussion of foodways would be complete without a consideration of the contexts in which food and beverage consumption took place. The sharing and consuming of food and beverages reinforced bonds between households, first for most African societies, and later for enslaved communities. Food was shared at religious or ceremonial events between the living and the dead, reinforcing ties between lateral and descending kin.

Many travelers' accounts from West Africa emphasize that ritual practices involved gifts of food and beverage to ancestors or deities. Family shrines located in house-yards featured food and beverage offerings as well. In his early twentieth century studies of the Ashanti, Rattray (1979:96) describes dishes of mashed yam and mashed plantain (*eto*) being offered to ancestors and other spirits in ceremonial contexts. Benne seed was used in a number of ceremonial contexts as well. Among the Bura peoples, benne seed was thrown over the shoulder to prevent evil or put in a *habtu* (a pot used for ceremonial purposes) to bring good luck (Meek 1931:164). In Sierra Leone, benne seed was used as part of a ritual punishment in Poro-Sande cultures. Differing degrees of punishment were inflicted upon those who were found guilty of some wrong by the society. A serious crime perpetuated against the community, such as theft, resulted in the perpetrator being required to pick up a quart of benne seed that had been poured on the ground by the elder. Creel (1988:181–82) describes how this ritual was carried on within the Praise houses of the Sea Island Gullah. Did a similar tradition become part of Bahamian life at any time?

Feasting was an important part of West African ritual life. Cruickshank reported (1853:187): "we find the natives keeping general feasts at stated times, which are likewise a part of their religion." Cruickshank describes Gold Coast feasts to celebrate the first fruits of the harvest, as well as feasts in which offerings of corn bread mixed with palm oil were made to the fish to ensure an abundant catch (Cruickshank 1853:188). Among the Yoruba, the yam harvest is a time of great celebration (Ojo 1966:231). In the

American South, annual cycles of planting and harvest became important, chronological landmarks for enslaved peoples. In Louisiana, the laborious sugar-grinding season was also a time of improved rations of food and alcohol. Christmas also became a time noted more for its feasting than its religious significance (Genovese 1974). Such occasions were often marked by the slaughter and sharing of a hog and other animals.

Rites of passage, such as marriage and coming-of-age ceremonies were often marked with food and drink. The Nankanse of Ghana used beer in coming-of-age head shaving ceremonies, female circumcisions, wedding ceremonies, ceremonies accompanying the distribution of meat after a successful hunt, ceremonies to ensure successful harvests, the dedication of religious shrines, curing rituals, funeral rites, and even rituals to cleanse murderers (Rattray 1932). Cruickshank (1853:192, 194) indicated that on the Gold Coast, betrothals were marked by gifts of rum to the bride's family. Additional gifts of rum, tobacco, and pipes were given by the husband to the wife's family before the marriage could be consummated. Rum was likewise used in naming ceremonies. Clear continuities in these practices can be seen in the American South, where rum or whiskey is often offered during weddings and funerals (Puckett 1926; Hyatt 1973; Rawick 1972).

Foods could also have healing powers—both physical and metaphysical. While the bush teas of the Caribbean have been well documented (e.g., Laguerre 1987, Jordan 1986; Grimé 1976), less consideration has been given to foods used in spiritually healing contexts. The Kilba are known to have incorporated benne seed into healing ceremonies, placing the seeds as offerings into pots designated as male and female to bring the two spiritual aspects back into harmony (Meek 1931:192). Cruickshank (1853:177) describes eggs being spattered on doorways and chickens being sacrificed as part of healing ceremonies in times of great illness among the Fanti. Ferguson (1992) has demonstrated that ritual healing was an important part of colonial African American practice on the eastern seaboard.

Foods and drinks could also have taboo qualities. In some cases, the proscriptions were temporary. For instance, as we discussed before, African women's activities were curtailed during menstruation. Among the Chamba groups of Nigeria, menstruating women were prevented from cooking. Cruickshank (1853:272) wrote: "Women are considered unclean at particular periods, and are not allowed to touch anything in the house or approach their husbands." Other taboos were of greater duration. Among peoples of the Gold Coast, Cruickshank (1853:144) stated that families could have particular foods named off limits to them as part of being associated with a particular deity. "And thus we will find one who will not taste a bit of chicken, another an egg, a turkey, and so on," with abstinence from that food being passed on to children.

Islamic food traditions also have strict food proscriptions. Given that Islam had spread to many West African regions by the time of the slave trade, we cannot rule out the possibility that members of the community were Muslim. Many of the meats available at Clifton would have fallen into forbidden categories for Muslim persons. For instance, pork is forbidden, as is goat and ox. Sheep is the most highly desired of the ruminants, which are favored over any other kind of food. According to the Koran fish is edible but not desirable, and there is debate among Muslim scholars as to the edibility of marine foods other than fish. Chicken is acceptable. While the zooarchaeological samples from Clifton are too small to explore food taboos, we must at least consider that the failure of some families on Clifton to raise pigs or chickens might arise from religious food concerns.

Whatever the nature of the specific rituals and practices incorporating food, it is clear that food was a means of communicating with the spiritual realm in a variety of ways. As part of that communication, communion between participants was also reinforced. The consumption of food, whether in a ceremonial context or not, could have provided a sense of community nurturing for the enslaved Africans of Clifton. Even in a secular setting, the sharing of a meal throughout a village is still a Bahamian tradition in the free African towns (Anderson 1998). We must consider the very real possibility that the foods cultivated and used at Clifton were intended to nourish the soul as well as the body.

CONCLUSIONS

The cooking style in the quarters of Clifton plantation demonstrates continuities between the cuisine of the American South, which had developed to meet the shortages of enslavement provisions, and the cooking practices of West Africa, which emphasized one-pot meals featuring chopped meats served from individual bowls and consumed with fingers or spoons. The ingredients available at Clifton would have been very familiar to people of either American or African birth, maximizing their ability to create beverages and foods true to African and African American cooking traditions. Iron pots, crocks, and African-style cooking features (hearths, etc.) would have made traditional cooking, brewing, and distilling practices easy to continue. We also see, however, innovation and adaptation in the diet. Wild birds and raccoon, a staple of North American enslaved people's diets, were also incorporated into meals, as were a host of locally available fish and shellfish. European ceramics were used to serve foods, but African and African American practices of collective dining were probably most commonly followed. We also see evidence that European wines, beers, and liquors were likely incorporated into the diet as well. Less evidence is available to suggest any kind of widespread interest in European relishes or pickles.

Food and beverages fed the soul and body alike: it is easy to imagine deceased and lost family members being recognized in the meals and observances of the community. The nature of the archaeological data also allows us to wonder if marriages, births, and deaths in the village continued to be commemorated with exchanges and offerings of food and drink.

For the people of Clifton, foodways would have been an important site of identity construction, for the technologies, ingredients, and etiquette associated with the procurement, preparation, and consumption of food at Clifton are widespread throughout much of West Africa. The shared practice of creating and consuming food together would have reinforced a sense of shared tradition and heritage among the diverse members of the plantation, whether their own immediate background was African, southern, or Bahamian Creole.

REFERENCES

Abrahams, R., and J. Szwed. 1983. *After Africa: Extracts from British Travel Accounts and Journals of the Seventeenth, Eighteenth, and Nineteenth Centuries concerning the Slaves, Their Manners, and Customs in the British West Indies.* New Haven: Yale University Press.

Agorsah, E. 1994. *Maroon Heritage: Archaeological, Ethnographic and Historical Perspectives.* Kingston: Canoe Press.

Anderson, N. 1998. Conversations and Excavations: An Ethnoarchaeological Examination of the African-Bahamian Houseyard. MA Thesis, Louisiana State University.

Armstrong, D. 1990. *The Old Village and the Great House.* Urbana: University of Illinois Press.

Bass, A. 1988. *Plain Southern Eating.* Durham: Duke University Press.

Bean, B. 1905. Fishes of the Bahama Islands. In *The Bahamas Islands*, ed. G. Shattuck, 294–328. New York: Johns Hopkins Press.

Berns, M. 1988. Ga'anda Scarification: A Model for Art and Identity. In *Marks of Civilization: Artistic Transformations of the Human Body*, ed. A. Rubin, 57–76. Los Angeles: UCLA Museum of Cultural History.

Bosman, W. 1814. A New and Accurate Description of the Coast of Guinea Divided into the Gold, the Slave, and the Ivory Coast. In *A General Collection of the Best and Most Interesting Voyages and Travels in All Parts of the World*, ed. J. Pinkerton, 337–538. London: Longman, Hurst, Rees, Orme and Brown.

Clarke, R. 1843. *Sierra Leone. A Description of the Manners and Customs of the Liberated Africans; with Observations upon the Natural History of the Colony and a Notice of the Native Tribes*. London: James Ridgway.

Colonial Office Record [CO] 23/63/16. 1812. Answers of William Wylly to Questions Posed by Committee of House of Assembly. National Archives, Kew, England.

CO 23/63/292–307. 1811. African List on Service of the Customs, Port of Nassau. National Archives, Kew, England.

CO 23/67/153–60. 1815. Regulations for the Government of the Slaves at Clifton and Tusculum in New Providence. National Archives, Kew, England.

CO 23/67/103–12. 1818. Letter. Munnings to Bathurst. National Archives, Kew, England.

CO 23/67/147–53. 1818. Letters. Wylly to Munnings. Enclosure, Munnings to Bathurst. National Archives, Kew, England.

CO 23/67/164–65. 1818. Encl. Letter, Rutherford to Wylly, in Munnings to Bathurst. National Archives, Kew, England.

Conneau, T. 1976. *A Slaver's Log Book or 20 Years' Residence in Africa*. Englewood Cliffs: Prentice-Hall.

Corry, J. 1968 [1807]. *Observations upon the Windward Coast of Africa: The Religion, Character, Customs, etc. of the Natives*. London: Frank Cass.

Craton, M., and D. Saunders. 1992. *Islanders in the Stream: A History of the Bahamian People, Volume One*. Athens: University of Georgia Press.

Creel, M. 1988. *"A Peculiar People": Slave Religion and Community-Culture among the Gullahs*. New York: New York University Press.

Cruickshank, B. 1966 [1853]. *Eighteen Years on the Gold Coast of Africa: Including an Account of the Native Tribes, and Their Intercourse with Europeans. Volume Two*. London: Frank Cass.

DeCorse, C. 2001. *An Archaeology of Elmina: Africans and Europeans on the Gold Coast, 1400–1900*. Washington, D.C.: Smithsonian Institution Press.

Deetz, J. 1993. *Flowerdew Hundred: The Archaeology of a Virginia Plantation, 1619–1864*. Charlottesville: University of Virginia Press.

Donnan, E. 1931. *Documents Illustrative of the History of the Slave Trade to America. Volume II: The Eighteenth Century*. Washington, D.C.: Carnegie Institution of Washington.

Durand, J. 1806. *Voyage to Senegal*. London: R. Phillips.

Eltis, D., S. Behrendt, D. Richardson, and H. Klein. 1999. *The Transatlantic Slave Trade*. Cambridge: Cambridge University Press.

Eneas, C. 1976. *Bain Town*. Nassau: Cleveland and Muriel Eneas.

Farnsworth, P. 1996. The Influence of Trade on Bahamian Slave Culture. *Historical Archaeology* 30(4):1–23.

Ferguson, L. 1992. *Uncommon Ground*. Washington, D.C.: Smithsonian Institution Press.

Finkelstein, J. 1978. Farming on Cat Island. In *Strangers no More: Anthropological Studies of Cat Island, the Bahamas*, ed. J. Savishinsky, 75–87. Ithaca: Department of Anthropology, Ithaca College.

Forde, D. 1951. *The Yoruba-Speaking Peoples of South-western Nigeria. Ethnographic Survey of Africa, Part IV, Western Africa*. London: International African Institute.

Franklin, M. 1997. Out of Site, Out of Mind: The Archaeology of an Enslaved Virginian Household, ca. 1740–1778. PhD diss., University of California, Berkeley.

———. 2001. The Archaeological Dimensions of Soul Food: Interpreting Race, Culture, and Afro-Virginian Identity. In *Race and the Archaeology of Identity*, ed. C. Orser Jr., 88–107. Salt Lake City: University of Utah Press.

Fries, E., ed. 1968. *Nassau, Bahamas 1823–4: Diary of a Physician from the United States Visiting the Island of New Providence*. Nassau: Bahamas Historical Society.

Genovese, E. 1974. *Roll, Jordan, Roll: The World the Slaves Made*. New York: Vintage Books.

Gomez, M. 1998. *Exchanging Our Country Marks: The Transformation of African Identities in the Colonial and Antebellum South*. Chapel Hill: University of North Carolina.

Goody, J. 1982. *Cooking, Cuisine and Class: A Study in Comparative Sociology*. Cambridge: Cambridge University Press.

Gray, W. 1825. *Travels in Western Africa, in the Years 1818, 19, 20, and 21, from the River Gambia, through Woolli, Bondoo, Galam, Kasson, Kaarta, and Foolidoo, to the River Niger*. London: John Murray.

Grimé, W. 1979. *Ethno-botany of the Black Americans*. Algonac, N.Y.: Reference Publications.

Hafner, D. 1993. *A Taste of Africa*. Berkeley, Calif.: Ten Speed Press.

Hauser, M., and D. Armstrong. 1999. Embedded Identities: Piecing Together Relationships through Compositional Analysis of Low-Fired Earthenwares. In *African Sites Archaeology in the Caribbean*, ed. J. Haviser, 65–93. Princeton: Markus Weiner Press.

Heath, B. 1999. Yabbas, Monkeys, Jugs, and Jars: An Historical Context for African-Caribbean Pottery on St. Eustatius. In *African Sites Archaeology in the Caribbean*, ed. J. Haviser, 196–220. Princeton: Markus Weiner Press.

Higman, B. 1998. *Montpelier Jamaica: A Plantation Community in Slavery and Freedom 1739–1912*. Barbados: The Press University of the West Indies.

Hultman. T., ed. 1985. *The Africa News Cookbook: African Cooking for Western Kitchens*. New York: Penguin Books.

Hyatt, H. 1973. *Hoodoo-Conjuration-Witchcraft-Rootwork*, vol. 3. St Louis: Western Publishing.

Jordan, P. 1986. *Herbal Remedies and Home Remedies: A Potpourri in Bahamian Culture*. Nassau: Nassau Guardian Printing Press.

Joyner, C. 1984. *Down by the Riverside: A South Carolina Slave Community*. Urbana: University of Illinois Press.

Keegan, W. 1997. *Bahamian Archaeology*. Nassau: Media Publishing.

Laguerre, M. 1987. *Afro-Caribbean Folk Medicine*. South Hadley, Mass.: Bergin and Garvey.

Lambert, R. 1990. *A Little Bahamian Cookbook*. Belfast: Appletree Press.

Lewicki, T., and M. Johnson. 1974. *West African Food in the Middle Ages According to Arabic Sources*. London: Cambridge University Press.

Littlefield, D. 1981. *Rice and Slaves: Ethnicity and the Slave Trade in Colonial South Carolina*. Baton Rouge: Louisiana State University Press.

Malone, S., and R. Roberts. 1991. *Nostalgic Nassau: Picture Postcards 1900–1940*. Nassau: A. C. Graphics.

Meek, C. 1931. *Tribal Studies in Northern Nigeria*. 2 vols. London: Kegan Paul, Trench, Trubner.

———. 1950. *A Sudanese Kingdom: An Ethnographical Study of the Jukun-Speaking Peoples of Nigeria*. New York: Humanities Press.

Miller, G. 1905. Mammals of the Bahamas Islands. In *The Bahamas Islands*, ed. G. Shattuck, 372–82. New York: Johns Hopkins Press.

Mintz, S. 1997. *Tasting Food, Tasting Freedom: Excursions into Eating, Culture, and the Past*. Boston: Beacon Press.

Mullin, M. 1992. *Africa in America: Slave Acculturation and Resistance in the American South and the British Caribbean 1736–1831*. Urbana: University of Illinois Press.

Mullins, P. 1999. *Race and Affluence: An Archaeology of African America and Consumer Culture*. New York: Kluwer Academic Press.

O'Connor, Terry. 2000. *The Archaeology of Animal Bones.* College Station: Texas A and M University Press.

Ojo, G. 1966. *Yoruba Culture: A Geographical Analysis.* London: University of Ife Press.

Park, M. 2000. *Travels in the Interior Districts of Africa*, ed. K. Marsters. Durham: Duke University Press.

Peggs, A. 1957. *A Relic of Slavery: Farquharson's Journal for 1831–32.* Nassau: The Deans Peggs Research Fund.

———. 1960. *A Mission to the West India Islands: Dowson's Journal for 1810–17.* Nassau: The Deans Peggs Research Fund.

Petersen, J., D. Watters, and D. Nicholson. 1999. Continuity and Syncretism in Afro-Caribbean Ceramics from the Northern Lesser Antilles. In *African Sites Archaeology in the Caribbean*, ed. J. Haviser, 157–95. Princeton: Markus Wiener.

Posnansky, M. 1999. West Africanist Reflections on African-American Archaeology. In *"I, Too, Am America": Archaeological Studies of African-American Life*, ed. T. Singleton, 21–38. Charlottesville: University of Virginia Press.

Price, S., and R. Price. 1980. *Afro-American Arts of the Suriname Rain Forest.* Berkeley: University of California Press.

Puckett, N. 1926. *Folk Beliefs of the Southern Negro.* New York: Greenwood Publishing.

Puckett, N., and M. Heller, eds. 1975. *Black Names in America: Origins and Usage.* Boston: G. K. Hall.

Rattray, R. 1932. *The Tribes of the Ashanti Hinterland.* 2 vols. Oxford: Clarendon Press.

———. 1979 [1927]. *Religion and Art in Ashanti.* New York: AMS Press.

Rawick, G. 1972. *From Sundown to Sunup.* Westport: Greenwood Press.

Reitz, E. 1994. Zooarchaeological Analysis of a Free African Community: Gracia Real de Santa Teresa de Mosé. *Historical Archaeology* 28(1):23–40.

Richardson, D. 1989. Slave Exports from West and West-Central Africa, 1780–1810: New Estimates of Volume and Distribution. *Journal of African History* 30:1–22.

Sambrook, P. 1996. *Country House Brewing in England 1500–1900.* London: Hambledon Press.

Saugnier, M. 1792. *Voyages to the Coast of Africa Containing an Account of the Shipwreck on Board Different Vessels and Subsequent Slavery, and Interesting Details on the Manners of the Arabs of the Desert, and of the Slave Trade, as Carried on at Senegal and Galam.* London: G. G. J. and J. Robinson.

Saunders, D. 1985. *Slavery in the Bahamas, 1648–1838.* Nassau: Nassau Guardian.

———. 1998. William Wylly and His Slaves at Clifton Plantation. *Journal of the Bahamas Historical Society* 20:27–33.

Saxon, L., E. Dreyer, and R. Tallant, eds. 1987. *Gumbo Ya-Ya: Folk Tales of Louisiana.* Gretna, La.: Pelican Publishing.

Schoepf, J. 1911. *Travels in the Confederation [1783–1784]. Vol. II: Pennsylvania, Maryland, Virginia, the Carolinas, East Florida, the Bahamas.* Philadelphia: William J. Campbell.

Scott, E. 1997. A Little Gravy in the Dish and Onions in a Tea Cup: What Cookbooks Reveal about Material Culture. *International Journal of Historical Archaeology* 1(2):131–56.

Weismantle, M. 2001. *Food, Gender, and Poverty in the Ecuadorian Andes.* Prospect Heights, Ill.: Waveland.

Wilkie, L. 2001. Methodist Intentions and African Sensibilities: The Victory of African Consumerism over Planter Paternalism at a Bahamian Plantation. In *Island Lives: Historical Archaeologies of the Caribbean,* ed. P. Farnsworth, 272–300. Tuscaloosa: University of Alabama Press.

Wilkie, L., and P. Farnsworth. 1999. Trade and the Construction of Bahamian Identity: A Multiscalar Exploration. *International Journal of Historical Archaeology* 3(4):283–320.

Wing, E., and E. Reitz. 1982. Prehistoric Fishing Economies of the Caribbean. *Journal of New World Archaeology* 5(2):13–32.

Winterbottom, T. 1969 [1803]. *An Account of the Native Africans in the Neighborhood of Sierra Leone to Which is Added an Account of the Present State of Medicine among Them.* Vol. 1. London: Frank Cass.

Black Seminole Diaspora: The Caribbean Connection

Rosalyn Howard

While conducting research on Andros Island, Bahamas, in 1937, archaeologist John Goggin met seventy-six-year-old Felix MacNeil. MacNeil told Goggin that he was the grandson of Scipio Bowlegs, a Seminole Indian bush medicine doctor who was among the first settlers of Red Bays, a Bahamian community on the northwestern coast of Andros Island. Like many others, MacNeil's family was forced to leave the original Red Bays settlement after it was devastated by several hurricanes. The family relocated to the northeast coastal settlement of Mastic Point. Goggin's journal entry reads as follows: "Tues., July 6 [1937] at Mastic Point, Andros Island: . . . Later went down to the water and sat under a big almond tree where a Negro named MacNeil was making a sculling oar. Spent the rest of the day there talking. MacNeil is from Red Bay and is part Indian" (Goggin 1937). MacNeil's grandfather, Scipio Bowlegs, was among the estimated 150 to 200 Black Seminoles who migrated to Andros Island from Florida.

This Caribbean connection to the Black Seminole diaspora is not widely known. Journal articles written by Kenneth W. Porter (1945) and John Goggin (1946) were among the few accounts referencing the legendary "wild Indians" of Andros Island. Twenty years earlier Bahamian journalist Mary Moseley (1926:66) wrote in her *Bahamas Handbook*, "It is to be hoped that the mystery of the interior of this [Andros] island will some day be unfathomed by means of aviation, when the allegations of explorers as to the existence of a tribe of people who hunt with bows and arrows can be investigated." Like Moseley, both Porter and Goggin believed that this was a topic worth exploring. As Goggin stated, "A more thorough study of the

Red Bay settlement would be interesting from many points of view and is certainly a worthy project" (Goggin 1946:206).

The westward path of the Black Seminole diaspora to Indian Territory (now Oklahoma) in the United States has been explored in several scholarly works (e.g., Mulroy 1993; Porter 1996; Katz 1986). However, in-depth examinations of the eastward Black Seminole diaspora to the Bahamas have been substantially missing from the scholarly record.[1] No extensive scholarly investigation was done on this "worthy project" until 1996 when I began my research. This essay presents an overview of the first substantial ethnohistory of the Caribbean connection of the Black Seminoles of Florida. Through information gleaned from archival documents and secondary sources, as well as the oral histories of descendants, a clearer portrait emerges of the diaspora called Black Seminoles: their exodus from Florida to long-sought freedom in the Bahamas and their continuous reinvention of identity and community in the Bahamas.

BLACK SEMINOLES IN FLORIDA

In 1693 a Royal Spanish decree promised sanctuary to all enslaved persons who reached St. Augustine, Florida, on the condition that they adopt the Catholic religion. Africans who had been enslaved on the plantations of southeastern North America, particularly in the neighboring Carolinas and Georgia, eagerly sought a new life of freedom in Spanish Florida. The Spanish granted these newly freed Africans plots of land two miles north of St. Augustine, where they established the first legally sanctioned black community in North America: *Gracia Reál de Santa Teresa de Mosé*, also known as Fort Mosé. However, greater than their concern for the spiritual well being of these Africans, or respect for their humanity, was the Spaniards' urgent need to defend themselves against invasions by U.S. citizens and troops. By offering enslaved Africans sanctuary, the Spanish could simultaneously bolster their defenses and undermine the stability of the plantation system that was threatening to overtake their sovereign territory, Florida.

Not all of the runaway Africans joined the Spaniards, however. Many of them joined forces with the Seminole Indians.[2] In most historical accounts these Africans are considered to be "slaves" of the Seminoles. It was however, a very different kind of association, more analogous to peonage or tenant farming than the chattel slavery suffered on the plantations. The Africans were only required to pay a portion of their harvests to the Seminole leaders and enjoyed substantial autonomy in their own separate communities known as "Black Towns." By the 1820s, an estimated four hundred Africans were associated with the Seminoles and appeared to be "wholly independent, without regard for the authority of their so-called masters, and [were described as 'slaves' only] in name" (Humphreys 1826:66).

The African-Seminole alliance stemmed from a mutual interest in securing their Florida haven. Seminole Indians fought to retain their land and livelihood, while Africans fought against a return to enslavement. It was this alliance that led to a new identity for the Africans as "Black Seminoles." Their ethnogenesis was forged in the crucible of radical sociocultural and sociopolitical change in Florida.

Although the Black Seminoles had escaped the plantations, they could not escape the persistent harassment of Euroamericans and their Native American allies. At the end of the First Seminole War in 1819, the United States annexed the Spanish territory of Florida and the colonists' migration there accelerated. The principal goal of the Euroamerican plot to annex Florida was to eliminate the significant threat to the institution of slavery that Spanish-controlled Florida represented. The eventual displacement of the majority of Seminoles from Florida to Indian Territory had much to do with their harboring escaped Africans who were described as fierce and intelligent warriors. General Jesup, in fact, described the Seminole Wars as being more accurately "Negro and Seminole wars" (Littlefield 1977:15).

Pushed further south by the influx of colonists and unfavorable treaty negotiations, Seminole Indians and Black Seminoles became maroons, taking refuge in the swamps and hammocks of southern Florida. Seminole leaders, desperate for assistance in their struggle against the Euroamerican aggressors, reached a consensus that tribal elder Chief Kenadgie should travel to New Providence (Bahamas) in an effort to solicit the assistance promised to them by the British. Seminoles and Black Seminoles had demonstrated their loyalty to the British during the siege of New Orleans. On September 29, 1819, Chief Kenadgie arrived on New Providence Island via dugout canoe accompanied by several others, including an interpreter described as "an Indian of mixed blood." That interpreter may have been Abraham, a Black Seminole who spoke several languages and who often negotiated with the Euroamericans on behalf of the Seminoles. The British, however, reneged on their promises. A peace treaty they had recently signed with the United States of America motivated their disinclination to interfere in the Seminoles' current dispute (Munnings 1980). Chief Kenadgie and his fellow travelers were provided with food and shelter on New

Providence for one week and summarily returned to Florida. Another party of ten Seminole Indians arrived in Nassau, New Providence, two years later in 1821, destitute and in need of food and clothing. Once again, the British leaders offered only provisions to the Seminoles before returning them to Florida.

Several months after the second group of Seminole Indians returned to Florida, a third group departed for the Bahamas. The majority of this group possibly consisted of Black Seminoles. They secretly congregated at Cape Florida (now Biscayne Bay) and embarked in whatever transport they could secure, whether dugout canoes or wreckers. "Wreckers" were ships engaged in searching for and salvaging wrecked cargo vessels—a lucrative business along the Florida coast at that time due to a lack of lighthouses. An estimated 150 to 200 persons made the journey to freedom between 1821 and 1837. Ethnohistorian Harry Kersey describes their exodus as "an epic journey born of desperation which has a modern counterpart in the Haitian and Cuban 'boat people'"(quoted in Flagg 2000:234).

The Seminoles' previous trips to the Bahamas had clearly demonstrated the futility of efforts to secure aid from the British on New Providence, so they altered their strategy. This third time they chose to land on the western shore of Andros Island, a large Out Island of the Bahamas approximately 25 miles west of New Providence and 150 miles southeast of the Florida coast. According to the oral history, they first landed at Cedar Coppitt ("coppitt" is Bahamian vernacular for "coppice," a densely wooded area) and then, later, traveled approximately fifteen miles north to the northwestern tip of the island, where they established the settlement of Red Bays.[3]

BLACK SEMINOLES IN THE BAHAMAS

Red Bays, where the critical mass of Black Seminole descendants resides today, is located three miles south of the original settlement. Contemporary Red Bays was originally called Lewis Coppitt because the Lewis family had purchased a large plot of land there; it was renamed approximately thirty years ago to honor the memory of their ancestors. By choosing the remote, northwestern coast of Andros Island, an area covered with dense pineyards ("coppitts") and bordered by shallow waters, the Black Seminoles finally achieved the sanctuary and freedom they had so long sought. All of them, however, did not remain in this area that they christened Red Bays. From there, some of them traveled southeastwardly along the shoreline, scattering throughout Andros Island in Nicholls Town, Lowe Sound,

Conch Bay, Mastic Point, Staniard Creek, Calabash Bay, and Fresh Creek, all settlements in north and central Andros Island, as well as the south Andros settlements of Mangrove Cay, Driggs Hill, and Long Bay. Their descendants are currently scattered throughout the Bahamas. The focus of my fieldwork was the Red Bays settlement, where I lived for one year while conducting this research.

They were a mysterious group, these Black Seminoles and their Bahamian-born descendants in Red Bays. With the exception of an influx of men who occasionally came from other islands to engage in the sponging industry, they were virtually isolated in Red Bays for almost 150 years. The community was accessible only by boat or footpath through dense coppitts until 1968, when the Owens Illinois logging company cut a road through the bush in order to harvest cut trees. Although the new road created unprecedented access into Red Bays, travel by automobile remained rather difficult until the late 1980s, when the road was finally paved. This relative isolation created an endogamous community in which many of these families intermarried. Not surprisingly, most people in Red Bays are closely related. The surnames Newton, Russell, Bowlegs, Miller, Colebrooke, and Marshall predominate among the Black Seminole descendants still residing on Andros Island in Red Bays, Lowe Sound, and Nicholls Town.

ORAL TRADITION

The Bahamian Black Seminoles descendants' understanding of the past and their relationship to it is contextualized in their social memory, the collective oral accounts that have been passed down through the generations. Following are excerpts from interviews that I recorded with consultants from several Andros Island communities who traced their Black Seminole heritage to the original settlers. Their oral tradition is relatively consistent and emphasizes the fundamental courage and tenacity of those Black Seminoles whose journey originated long ago on Georgia and South Carolina plantations and in the Black Towns of the Florida Seminoles.

THE REVEREND BERTRAM A. NEWTON—RED BAYS

Bertram A. Newton was born in and has lived in Red Bays for all but one of his seventy-nine years.[4] He spent that year away from home while attending Teachers College in Nassau. He returned to become the teacher and principal of Red Bays All-Age School (later named Red Bays Primary

School). "Teacher," as Rev. Newton is affectionately known in Red Bays, credits Pastor Joseph Lewis, whose grandfather Sammy Lewis was an original Red Bays settler, as the source of most of the information contained in the booklet he wrote in 1968 entitled *A History of Red Bays, Andros, Bahamas*. Rev. Newton is a community leader. In addition to being the former principal and teacher of the school for forty-one years, he is the pastor of the settlement's only church—New Salem Baptist. Rev. Newton is very proud of his heritage and views the project of recording the oral tradition of Red Bays as "very, very important for the oncoming generation, say, like my grandchildren and like the great-grand that will come after." He adds that, "when I think back on the history, I think that I'm a millionaire."[5]

Rev. Newton traced his lineage to the original settlers through his paternal great-grandfather and maternal great-grandmother. Rev. Newton related to me that

> I am the son of Rev. Eldrack Eneas Newton and Adranna Newton Dean [who was] born at Red Bays. Eldrack Newton was born in Staniard Creek Andros, that's Central Andros. He was the son of Arthur Newton, [who was] the son of Moses Newton, one of the Seminole Indians who came from Florida about 1845.[6] Eldrack Newton was born in 1900 and went to the [World] War in 1914. After he came from the War, he had nothing to do. He came down sponging at Red Bays, saw Adranna, marry her, settle here. Adranna was the granddaughter of Mary Lewis, also a Seminole Indian that came from Florida with her brothers and those, [such as] Watkin Lewis and her father Sammy Lewis. They have had together, well, my mother told me 18 children and I was about the second. But only nine were known to live.

Rev. Newton and others among the Black Seminole descendants use the term "Seminole" when referring to their ancestors, rather than "Black Seminole." Apparently, their ancestors did not distinguish themselves in the manner that outsiders did, based upon a dichotomous racial typology.

THE REVEREND BENJAMIN LEWIS—RED BAYS

Benjamin Lewis was a seventy-six-year-old retired seaman and construction worker when I interviewed him. He died on February 14, 2005, after serving for many years as the Associate Pastor of Red Bays' New Salem Baptist Church. Rev. Lewis left Red Bays as a young man and worked in Nassau as a carpenter for twenty years. It was during this time that his father, Joseph Lewis, related the history of Red Bays to Bertram Newton.

Benjamin Lewis returned home after his father became ill and he subsequently remained in Red Bays after his father's death at age eighty-four. Rev. Lewis remembered:

> He [Joseph Lewis] let me know that I'm a part of the Seminole Indians. My great-grandfather was Sammy Lewis, which was his grandfather. He came from Florida in a canoe and the first place they rested was at Cedar Coppitt. Later on down, they move from Cedar Coppitt and they went up into a lake and they came into a little island and he fall in love with the little island, and he give it name Sammy Lewis after him.
>
> He stood there for while, and after [that] he thought it is fit that he travel someplace else. He start traveling down north till he reach a place down here which he call Red Bay. And he was there until an hurricane came, and this hurricane overflow the place. And they leave from there and they came up here to the place call Lewis Coppitt. He purchased 61 and 3 quarter acre ground and give it name Lewis Coppitt. And the Lewises were the first to settle here in this little part of Andros, which is the last tip of North Andros call Red Bay. But this place [today's Red Bays] is formerly known as Lewis Coppitt. And he preside here and he raise up his sons and daughters and after departure of the old man Sammy Lewis, then Watkin Lewis and his children stood here. And later on there are some others come in and join with them and make this to become a settlement.
>
> We the people of Red Bay we give God the glory for the old patriarch Sammy Lewis who had made preparation for this coming generation. And that is why we, the Lewises people, is call the Seminole descent.

Rev. Lewis's family still holds claim to the largest amount of land owned in present day Red Bays. His great-grandfather, Sammy Lewis, is named on the roster of "97 Foreign Negro Slaves" in an 1828 letter to the Governor from the British Customs officer who seized and transported them to Nassau (Grant 1828). Sammy Lewis and seven of his brothers were among the first settlers from Florida.

WILLIAM COLEBROOKE—RED BAYS

"Old Iron," or "Scrap Iron," as William Colebrooke is known to most local people, is sixty-eight years of age. Like most other men in Red Bays, he earned his livelihood on the sea until a few years ago, when someone stole his boat. Occasionally, he still goes out to sea, fishing with other men from the settlement, and he makes crabbing trips in season. As a rule he is a solitary character. Old Iron now makes his living predominantly by sewing baskets. He is noted for sewing some of the largest baskets ever crafted in Red Bays, including the one he made for me that measures 34 inches in height and 160 inches in circumference. He often served as my guide; we biked three miles through the bush, mostly along an overgrown former logging road, to the site of the original Red Bays settlement. Old Iron told me that:

> In the years past, when the war was on, the people, the Seminolians from Florida, travel by canoes from Florida and the first place they end up was Big Cross Cay, then come into Red Bay. And from Red Bay they settle there for a while. Some of them stop at Red Bay and some of them travel on from Cedar Coppitt to go down the shore as far as come round up to Driggs Hill, Behring Point, come round Mangrove Cay, Long Bay Cay, and all of them, and come straight up round there to on the east side of Andros. Maybe some may gone into Nassau, I don't know.
>
> RH: Were your great-grandparents some of the original settlers?
> WC: Um-hum, such as Mary Russell, Pa Watkin, and amongst them. And John Lewis, Shaddy [Shadrack] Lewis, and so on. When a hurricane come down the place flood and they move from there [original Red Bays site] and come up to Red Bay . . . this place now. At first they call it Lewis Coppitt because one set of the Lewis was here first, and the other set was down to Red Bay. Then the main boss who was over all of them come up here, then all decide to live at Lewis Coppitt. Then after all the old folks dead out, then [Rev.] B. A. Newton say we'll change the name from Lewis Coppitt to Red Bay. That's how this place get to call Red Bay. This place is not [the original] Red Bay. This happen in the early part. What time I can't remember. My great-grandma, Ma Mary, all of them come from Florida.

His nicknames, Old Iron or Scrap Iron, likely emanate from his tough persona. His weathered hands and face speak volumes, acknowledging years of hard work on the sea, catching and spearing fish and sponges, as well as hunting land crabs in season. Despite this, his tall, lean frame belies his chronological age. He is a fiercely proud man, especially when speaking of "de Seminolians dem," his ancestors.

THE REVEREND FREDERICK RUSSELL—RED BAYS

Frederick Russell, sixty-eight years old at the time I interviewed him in 1996, died in 1999. He was born and raised in Red Bays. For many years he served as a deacon in Red Bays' New Salem Baptist Church, and at the time of his death he was the pastor of Mizpah Baptist Church in Nicholls Town. Russell was one of only few older-generation Red Bays residents who received any formal education beyond primary school. By his own admission, Russell may not have known the history as well as Rev. Bertram Newton:

> I spend a majority of my life off from here, in Nassau. I was a train nurse at the Princess Margaret Hospital. I grew up here, I had my education here in the All-Age School, called E. E. Newton All-Age School. The highest grade was then grade four and I went through grade four. After I left school I went to Nassau. I was then nineteen years old. My father name was Joshua Shadrack Russell and my mother name was Leanora Russell and they both are dead now. They were very poor people. They was a part of the Seminole Indians descendant. My father, his mother was a sister of the Lewis, Sam Lewis, who was an Indian. He came here from Florida I heard, and my daddy was one of her sons. He got married to my mother, Leanora Newton from Staniard Creek.
>
> . . . it was couple a those brothers, it was Sam those men, I heard, came from there [Florida] in a boat, in a canoe. My mother['s] father, or my grandfather, was also an Indian [Moses Newton]. They [the Lewises] had Indian blood and one stop into Mastic Point I think, and so on, but they separate themselves from each others, and then they married, they get children, and all of they children become their generation, and so we call the whole body of Indians, the Seminole Indians, a generation.

As Rev. Russell states, some of the Black Seminole ancestors made their homes in communities other than Red Bays on Andros Island. Staniard Creek, Nicholls Town, Lowe Sound, Conch Sound, and Mastic Point are among the North Andros settlements where their descendants still reside. Rev. Russell's extended family in Red Bays has more members than any other. Children, grandchildren, and great-grandchildren, born both within and outside of wedlock, maintain close ties to one another. His brother Stancil, for example, has twenty-two children that he fathered with two women in Red Bays. This endogamous proclivity, certainly not limited to the Russells, is likely a result of the relative isolation of Red Bays for such a long period of time. It is also possibly due to an imbalance in the gender ratio. Rev. Russell's great-grandfather, John Russell, is also listed among the ninety-seven people seized and taken to Nassau in 1828.

ALMA (PRUDENCE) MILLER—LOWE SOUND

I encountered Alma Miller, sixty-nine years young, tending her small garden when I approached her house. Like Rev. Russell, she is also now deceased.

Skillfully wielding a cutlass, she chopped the weeds away from her small crop of cassava, eddy (local name for the edible root of the eddo plant, commonly found in the tropics), and corn in the yard next to her house. She welcomed me into her home, eager to share with me what she remembered about her Seminole Indian heritage. In Alma Miller's words:

> My family told me that in the slavery times, my foreparents were run away on a raft from Florida. And they come into Bahamas. They was my foreparents, great-grands . . . Alice and Isaac Miller. But their first stop then was in Eleuthera. And one set had a family that stop by Cedar Coppitt [Andros], and therefore they make a home from there come through with the people and them Indian and whatever. And Granddaddy went up in Eleuthera and they buy a lot a land up in there. And they come here [to Andros] and they buy a lot a land down here [in Lowe Sound] and about, in the swashes. [In] Eleuthera they open up a pineapple farm, and they had a sheep farm, and they had a beef farm up in Eleuthera. So the family scatter from Eleuthera and Andros and on South Andros.
>
> Now them set what come over, I can't tell whether they been African or they's a pure blood of Indian. I know they was a Indian family, they was Indian blood. But just know when I be young and be traveling [in Florida] and the Indian they begin owning me, as a part of them. Sometime I see them right here in Nassau. They come over on trips and I go in the States the same thing. I go New York, the same thing, no different. Just when I buck one of them, they own me, they hold me up.

Alma Miller was a tall, "bright" (light-brown skinned), striking woman; it is easy to understand why, in younger years, she bore the nickname "Andros Glamour." As we sat down to commence our interview, she loosed her bound-up, straight black hair and it flowed past her shoulders. She was anxious to display her "Indian hair," as she called it, as a sign of authenticity.

CHARLES BOWLEGS—NICHOLLS TOWN

Charles Bowlegs, in his fifties, lives in Nicholls Town and is readily identified by Bahamians as "Indian" because he is "bright" and has high cheekbones. He is a member of the Bowlegs family that has long-established roots in Nicholls Town. His niece, Michele Bowlegs, is currently the principal of the Red Bays Primary School. Charles Bowlegs told me that he learned the story of the Black Seminole exodus to the Bahamas from his grandaunt, Blossom Bowlegs:

> She was Blossom Bowlegs until she got married to Evans. Her parents came from the west coast of Andros. Her grandparents came from Florida, and they landed on the west coast at a place call Cedar Coppitt. Her grandparents told her that after they come over, they find on the north side was a much better place, higher ground. Then they went back and get the family, and come on the north side [Nicholls Town].
>
> I never knew my great-grandmother, I never recognize her name, but I heard she was mixed with Indian blood, light-skinned. I used to go to Florida a lot when I was much younger and I run into several people who told me that they bears the same title [surname], Bowlegs.

The surname "Bowlegs" is the only one of Seminole origin that survives among the Black Seminole descendants in the Bahamas. Many of the Bowlegs live in Nicholls Town, but there are others in South Andros and in Nassau. Charles likes to tell the humorous story of an occasion when he was temporarily detained by Florida immigration officers. Upon presenting his identification, the examining officer went behind closed doors and returned with another officer, a light-skinned man whose name was also Bowlegs. He joked with Charles about the fact that there are white ones and black ones, too. The Bowlegs family has long been influential in Nicholls Town, owning businesses and involved in politics. Charles Bowlegs's uncle, Herbert, was the oldest living Bowlegs family member until his death in 2003.

OMELIA MARSHALL—RED BAYS

At eighty-five years of age, Omelia Marshall, affectionately known as "Mama" or "Meena" or respectfully addressed as "Miss Marshall," is considered the matriarch of Red Bays. She has been the bush medicine woman, a midwife, and tour guide in Red Bays since she was very young. We met on numerous occasions in what she calls "Marshall Town," a compound-style setting with several small houses and shacks set roughly in a circle—including a "Tatch Camp" that resembles a Seminole chickee—where she lives among three generations of family. According to Miss Marshall:

> The tatch camp built for hurricane. When the hurricane come down in Betsy Hurricane I had a big tatch camp [now only one structure stands].
>
> RH: So you're safer in the tatch camp than the house during a hurricane?

> OM: Yes ma'am, [I] tell you something, if hurricane come now, and you got a tatch camp you go right in there, and you catch fire in that, make up your bed, then you go and get some cassava. You bake your bread you boil your hot coffee. You laying down sleeping, the wind blowing or what have you.

The women of Marshall Town can be seen daily sewing baskets in the yard. Even a few of the small children sew too, proudly showing off their attempts at basketry. Miss Marshall's father, she says, was the first to start the basket-sewing tradition of Red Bays; he used sea grass and formed the baskets in one style—the fanner. She learned the craft from him, but improvised the style and materials. Now she and others in Red Bays sew baskets from palm "top" harvested from the surrounding pineyards.

Marshall Town is the main stop on tours of Red Bays, conducted mainly by Forfar Field Station staff who weekly bring students to hear Miss Marshall talk about Red Bays' history and culture. In acknowledgment of her service as a greeter who is always ready to demonstrate the ways that they used to grate cassava and coontie to make flour in the old days and who is always eager to retell the stories locked in her memory even at eighty years old as she strips the palm thatch preparing to sew a basket, she has received several awards commending her outstanding "hospitality" from the Bahamas Ministry of Tourism and others. She is very proud of these plaques and is quick to send one of the many children milling around Marshall Town into her house to retrieve them for viewing by visitors. Omelia Marshall recounts that:

> My great-granddaddy was Scipio Bowleg, and his son is Scipio Bowleg, and my daddy is Scipio Demeritte. My mother is Marion [Bowleg] Demeritte. She formerly from Red Bay, but my daddy from Lowe Sound. I come from Lowe Sound when I was nine years old, bathing in the sea, naked, nine years old. My grandmother name Marta Celeste Russell. My great-grandfather they say he leave from America Land where the Seminoles come from. Then when he come from there, he stop to Josie [Joulter] Cay. From Josie Cay he leave from there and he go down to Cedar Coppitt and build he house. He kitchen and he house foundation still there.

Miss Marshall's reference to "bathing in the sea, naked" is her way of expressing her innocence at such a young age and the uninhibited style of life back then. Her bush medicine skills were passed down in the family from her grandfather, Scipio Bowlegs, the bush medicine "doctor" who was also the grandfather of Felix MacNeil. As she states, there are still remains of the original houses at Cedar Coppitt, constructed by the first Black Seminoles to arrive on Andros Island. I discovered on a recent trip there that these old foundations are not in view from the shoreline, but are hidden amid mangroves, pine trees, and thatch plants. Cedar Coppitt is located approximately fifteen miles south of present day Red Bays.

These oral traditions have been passed down through the older generations in Red Bays but, unfortunately, are rarely repeated to the children today. The times when the community was very isolated, when stories of their heritage were repeated around fires that lit the pitch-dark nights are gone. Television, street lamps, individual telephones in their homes, and easy exit via paved roads are factors that have greatly changed the structure and nature of this community, thereby engendering the loss of their oral tradition.

Their Black Seminole ancestors had been living as free men and women for seven years in the original settlement of Red Bays before they encountered British authorities. In August of 1828, Port of Nassau Customs Officer Winer Bethell seized and delivered to the port of Nassau "ninety-seven foreign Negro slaves," taken from their homes on Andros Island under the mistaken belief that they had been "illegally imported" into Andros Island (one of the Bahama Islands) by Spaniards who had continued the slave trade long after the British abolished it in 1807 (Grant 1828). An 1828 letter in the Bahamas National Archives documents this seizure and lists the names of those seized. Several names on roster match those of the great-grandparents that my consultants related to me in our interviews, confirming the oral history that their ancestors were among the original settlers who escaped from Florida.

That 1828 customs report indicated that the persons seized had been living on Andros Island since 1821, "peacefully and quietly, and have supported themselves upon fish, conchs and crabs which are to be met in abundance and upon Indian corn, plantains, yams, potatoes and peas which they have raised." After reviewing their case in Nassau, Bahamian Governor J. Carmichael Smyth remarked that "the question of these people being considered as slaves illegally imported was not noted until they had already been settled here seven years and that during these seven years, there did not occur a single instance of any one of these Negroes being carried away to Cuba. I see therefore no grounds to suspect any improper motives on the part of the owners of the vessels who brought them from Florida; or to doubt the truth of the story told by the poor people themselves more particularly as many of them still have their discharges from His Majesty's service" (Smyth 1980). After almost one year of detention in Nassau, they were released and returned to their homes in Red Bays. The Black Seminoles had finally found freedom—in the Bahamas.

In February 2003, the first reunion of the Bahamian Black Seminole descendants and members of the Seminole Tribe of Florida occurred at the Seminole Tribal Fair on the Hollywood reservation near Ft. Lauderdale. The Bahamian Ministry of Tourism sponsored a small group from Red Bays to display and sell their baskets and woodcarvings. A few representatives of the Bahamian media and the Ministry of Tourism accompanied them. The media interviewed Seminole Tribe of Florida Chairman Mitchell Cyprus, and the Black Seminole descendants presented him with special gifts: a carving, created that day on the fairgrounds from a raw piece of mahogany wood, and one of the unique baskets for which Red Bays has become noted. This historic event received wide coverage on Bahamian television and radio and led to a new appreciation of the Black Seminole descendants. If this newly re-established relationship is nurtured, it may grow into a meaningful alliance of these descendants whose ancestors valiantly fought together against egregious odds on Florida soil.

The complex relationships forged between the Seminoles, the Black Seminoles, the British, and the Spaniards are significant with respect to the African diaspora in North America and the Caribbean. Their long-term contact led to intermarriage, trade activities, and war alliances in Florida, the Bahamas, and Cuba. Their history causes us to wrestle with contemporary assumptions about boundaries, both geographic and ethnic.

NOTES

1. The publications of Porter (1996:26) and Mulroy (1993:26) dedicate only a few sentences to the Black Seminoles' Caribbean connection.

2. In the Creek language "Seminole" means "runaways" (Giddings 1858:3). Others concur that "Seminole" means "wild" or "runaway," but argue instead that the name applies to Creeks who abandoned their territories in Alabama and Georgia and settled in Florida (Katz 1986, Littlefield 1977). "Seminole" is further speculated to be an adaptation from the Spanish *cimarron* meaning "wild one," which originally referred to domestic cattle that had taken to the hills in Hispaniola. Later on, it was associated with Native American slaves who had escaped from the Spaniards. Sturtevant (1971:110) suggests that the meaning of "Seminole" evolved into use as the collective name for all Florida Indians, despite the fact that they emanated from culturally and linguistically diverse Indian tribes or nations.

3. Some may have actually traveled around the southern tip of Andros after leaving Cedar Coppitt, establishing homes in the South Andros settlements Mangrove Cay, Driggs Hill, and Long Bay.

4. At the time of his birth, the area was known as "Lewis Coppitt."

5. The importance of recording this oral history was confirmed because two of my consultants quoted herein are now deceased.

6. This date may be incorrect. The 1828 Customs roster lists a "Moses" who was most likely Rev. Newton's great-grandfather. Moses is listed along with his brothers John and Stephen Newton (spelled "Nuton" on the roster).

REFERENCES

Bethell, W. 1828. London Duplicate Despatches. In *A Guide to Selected Sources for the History of the Seminole Settlements at Red Bays, Andros 1917–1980. Appendix 10*, ed. D. E. Wood. Nassau: Dept. of Archives.

Flagg, H. 2000. Black Indians of Red Bays. In *Bahamas Handbook*. Nassau, Bahamas: Etienne Dupuch Jr. Publications

Forbes, J. 1993. *Africans and Native Americans: The Language of Race and the Evolution of Red-Black Peoples*. Urbana: University of Illinois Press.

Giddings, J. 1858. *The Exiles of Florida: Or, the Crimes Committed by Our Government Against the Maroons, Who Fled from South Carolina and Other Slave States, Seeking Protection Under Spanish Laws*. Columbus, Ohio: Follett, Foster, and Company.

Goggin, J. 1937. Bahamas Journal Notes. P. Yonge Collection. University of Florida.

———. 1946. The Seminole Negroes of Andros Island, Bahamas. *Florida Historical Quarterly* 24:201–6.

Grant, L. 1828, June 30. CO23/78/58. Microfilm. Nassau, Bahamas: Bahamas National Archives.

Hudson, C., ed. 1971. *Red, White, and Black: Symposium on Indians in the Old South*. Athens: University of Georgia Press.

Humphreys, G. 1826. Humphreys to Acting Governor William McCarty. Territorial Papers of the United States. Vol. 23, p. 9. Cited in Blacks and the Seminole Removal Debate, 1821–1835, by G. Klos. *Florida Historical Quarterly* 66: 55–78.

Katz, W. 1986. *Black Indians: A Hidden Heritage*. New York: Atheneum.

Littlefield, D. 1977. *Africans and Seminoles from Removal to Emancipation*. Westport, Conn.: Greenwood Press.

Moseley, M. 1926. *The Bahamas Handbook*. Nassau: Nassau Guardian.

Mulroy, K. 1993. *Freedom on the Border: The Seminole Maroons in Florida, the Indian Territory, Coahuila, and Texas*. Lubbock: Texas Tech University Press.

Munnings, W. 1980 [1819, November 30]. Governor's Despatches 1818–1825. In *A Guide to Selected Sources for the History of the Seminole Settlements at Red Bays, Andros 1917–1980. Appendix 5*, ed. D. Wood. Nassau: Dept. Of Archives.

Porter, K. 1945. Notes on Seminole Negroes in the Bahamas. *Florida Historical Quarterly* 24(1):57–61.

———. 1996. *The Black Seminoles: History of a Freedom-Seeking People*. Gainesville, Fla.: University Press of Florida.

Smyth, J. 1980 [1831, August 10]. London Duplicate Despatches. In *A Guide to Selected Sources for the History of the Seminole Settlements at Red Bays, Andros 1817–1980, Appendix 13*, ed. D. Wood. Nassau: Bahamas Department of Archives.

Sturtevant, W. 1971. Creek into Seminole. In *North American Indians in Historical Perspective*, ed. E. B. Leacock and N. O. Lurie, 92–128. New York: Random House.

Woodson, C. 1920. The Relations of Negroes and Indians in Massachusetts. *Journal of Negro History* 5:44–57.

P. K. Yonge Collection. 1937. Bahamas Journal Notes. University of Florida.

Rockin' and Rushin' for Christ: Hidden Transcripts in Diasporic Ritual Performance

Joyce Marie Jackson

In the Bahamas the phrase "rushin' through the crowd" invokes Junkanoo for most insiders. Junkanoo is a secular celebration that takes place on the morning after Christmas. Its origin, however, is religious, as Rev. Bertran Newton (1996), the elderly statesman and minister of the Baptist church in Red Bays on Andros Island, informed me: "Rushin' started in the churches. Well I'm 70 years old and when I came on the scene I met rushin' after a church service and especially Christmas and New Year's. Rushin' was done in the church before the streets. I believe that rushin' was developed by Christian families and because it was done in the church, I further believe that those persons wanted some type of enjoyment for Christian people."

Correspondingly, when people in the northeast Delta section of Louisiana state that they are going to the "Rock," rock and roll is the default expectation for outsiders. In fact, they are referring to what is known as the Easter Rock, a religious ritual celebrating the resurrection of Christ. Mrs. Jimmie Lee Jones of Winsboro, Louisiana, recalls: "My mother explained to us what it was and let us know that it was sacred. It was our heritage and this was something that we did to remember the risen Savior. So, therefore you took it deep down inside and you did it with joy and pleasure because you were rocking to this. If you did it with foolishness or anything, the old people did not stand that in those days. They wanted you to be straight with what you were doing" (1996).

To understand these rituals and their significance in their respective church communities, I draw upon historical records and recent ethnographic field data and personal observations of a Rushin' ceremony in a Pentecostal church on Andros Island, Bahamas, and the Easter Rock ceremony in a Baptist church in Winnsboro, Louisiana. I have been researching the Easter Rock tradition since 1994, interviewing primarily elderly community members who have given me greater insight into the meanings and interpretations of various elements of the Rock. Both Rushin' and Easter Rock are centered around Christian holidays: Rushin' occurs during Christmas and New Year's and the Rock happens on the eve of Easter Sunday. Both of these rituals involve sacred music and the performance of variants of the "ring shout," a black religious dance usually done in a counterclockwise circular movement that has strong ties to African performance practices. Historically, a group or band of singers performed the dance in a circle, their feet never crossing and rarely lifting from the ground. Numerous accounts of the ring shout in the literature of the antebellum period (see also Epstein 1977; Levine 1977; Stuckey 1987; and Blassingame 1979) make clear its historical African antecedents. Performed in praise houses and slave quarters, the practice was passed on to the black folk church. Although my primary focus is not on African practices and symbolism, these cultural continuities cannot be ignored.

While a number of studies focus on African diasporic musical religious traditions, they seldom offer a gendered reading of power relations inherent in the performance of such musical rituals despite the prominence of women in both Rushin' and Rockin' ceremonies. To fill this void, in the following pages I examine women's roles as dynamic agents of growth, change, and continuity in two churches where these ceremonies are performed. In both places, the women shape and redefine their status on a symbolic level as well as within the actual organization, thereby gaining authority and power.

Within ritual musical performance women find agency in an otherwise male-dominated cultural system, providing an alternative theoretical lens through which to view authority and power within the "black folk church." Within these rituals black church women are not passive minions of black male church leadership but rather active agents in cultivating female authority through developing what James C. Scott calls "hidden transcripts" (1990). That this source of empowerment emerges within performance highlights the generative power of ritual often associated with diasporic traditions and illustrates how women exercise authority under different terms.

HISTORICAL PERSPECTIVES

Previous studies on the Easter Rock appear to consist of three articles and a brief mention of the ritual in a fourth. The earliest study, "Easter Rock: A Louisiana Negro Ceremony" by Lea and Marianna Seale (1942), describes the ritual as it was performed in the 1940s. The authors observed the ritual three times in two plantation churches and interviewed two of the oldest blacks living in Concordia Parish. Their opening statement, "An Easter rock is one of those pagan rites clothed in Christian symbolism which are not altogether uncommon among the Negroes of the South" (1942:212), immediately reveals the biases of that day and era. However, the article is valuable because it is the earliest primary account of the ritual and it includes song lyrics. The second article, "Easter Rock Revisited: A Study in Acculturation" by Harry Oster (1958), is the English professor's report of his 1956 observations of the Easter Rock ritual near Clayton, Louisiana, in Concordia Parish at one of the churches the Seales observed. He states, "Since the authors of the original article did not describe the African origins of certain features of the service, I shall trace the background out of which these primitive elements came" (1958:22). He does provide some background information that differs from that in the Seales's article, tying the Easter Rock vocalizations to the "shout," interpreting aspects of the ritual, speculating about African customs survivals, providing the text of a sermon and lyrics to songs, and discussing degrees of acculturation.

In "Africa in the Delta" by cultural geographer Hiram Gregory (1962), the Easter Rock is only briefly discussed for a page and a half: Gregory describes the Easter Rock ritual as a "prime example of acculturation" in the Louisiana Delta. His description provides another eyewitness account of the ritual at a later date and also in another area of the Delta: Gregory made observations at the Primitive African Baptist Church near Waterproof, Louisiana, and at the Pittsfield Plantation Church near Ferriday, Louisiana. His work thus indicates that the Easter Rock was not exclusive to one location in the Louisiana Delta. Although he recognized that the Easter Rock was "a stylized form of religious observance," he commented that the "dance is now vanishing rapidly from the Delta scene" (1962:17). However, I cannot agree with his assertion that "today the loss of meaning of the ritual is ample evidence of the changing status of culture" (1962:19). Gregory's inability to elicit adequate explanations of meaning from the participants at the ritual does not mean there are none.

It is clear that none of the authors of the three historical articles intended to study the Rock in depth, and this influenced their observations and descriptions of the Rock. Gregory, for example, claimed that, "adequate explanations are not given" (1962:18), which led him to the premature conclusion that "the results of the process of acculturation are now apparent. The African elements have fused with the Anglo-American elements. . . . The Easter Rock, now only a revered tradition, once was the mystic dance of the practitioners of voodoo" (1962:22). He provides absolutely no explanation or supporting evidence for this statement. In over a decade of researching this tradition, I have never heard any of the practitioners I have worked with mention Vodun in relation to the Easter Rock, not even people who spoke against the tradition. In fact, when I have asked practitioners about Vodun, they clearly indicate that it has nothing to do with the Rock. They are Baptist (Christian) and because Vodun is a traditional African-derived religion, they do not identify with its practices. Thus Gregory's attempt to link Easter Rock to Africa through Vodun is misguided, although African elements are present in the Louisiana Easter Rock. However, because "Voodoo" is a catchall phrase for African religious practices in the U.S. South, this may have been Gregory's way of acknowledging the differences or the perceived African origins of the ritual. The original African significance of the Easter Rock ritual may have long been forgotten, but the ceremony carries biblical meaning that is enduringly real and important to those who still participate in it.

Janet Sturman (1993), an ethnomusicologist, has published the third article that focuses entirely on the Easter Rock. Her article is based upon two years of participant observation of the annual Rock ritual in Clayton, Louisiana, in Concordia Parish. Along with providing a detailed description, history, and analysis of the Easter Rock tradition in that particular church, Sturman focuses on the role of assertion in contemporary efforts to revive the Easter Rock at that church. She contends that "the Easter Rock transforms the forbidden into the permissible and asserts an identity that paradoxically derives power from both dimensions" (1994:24). She uses the musical component of the ceremony to illustrate the layers of assertion that tend to keep the tradition alive. In analyzing the key spiritual "Walk Together Children" she argues that the lyrics of the spiritual, the performance practices of their delivery, and the sacred dancing that accompanies them collectively reveal an array of pasts. Therefore to participate is to "relive that past and to make it a source of power" (1994:31). My own observations and analysis support Sturman's contention that the Easter Rock transfers the forbidden into the permissible. Although the various churches have different key spirituals, their meanings are all similar, as are the performance practices and the accompanying dance or rock. As such, through collective cultural memory, the Easter Rock certainly asserts a source of power for the women who annually create and relive that past.

There is very little published on the Rushin' tradition. I first heard about rushin' in a Bahamian presentation at the 1995 Smithsonian Festival of American Folklife, where it was described as a "round dance in the church for funerals and other occasions." Since then, I have only found citations on the term rushin', or rushing, in conjunction with the secular Junkanoo tradition. In that tradition, the dance movement of festival participants in the streets is referred to as rushin'.

In 1995, while accompanying a documentary photographer on a photo shoot in the Bahamas focusing on the Junkanoo celebration in Nassau, I caught a glimpse of a tourism "infomercial" for Andros Island. Describing the Junkanoo rushin' in the streets of Nassau, the narrator commented that the practice had originated in the churches. The video also featured a brief interview with two participants and showed brief scenes from a church Rushin' event. I was able to acquire a copy of the tape and talk to the official who had produced the program for the Office of Tourism. I also interviewed people in Nassau about the tradition. This started my quest to learn more about the circular ritual in Bahamian churches. In 1996, I returned to the Bahamas specifically to conduct research on Andros Island.

Black folk church rituals, whether in the Bahamas or the United States, are characterized by the emotional and musical delivery style of sermons, the spontaneous verbal and nonverbal interaction of preachers and congregations, African-styled music transmitted through the oral tradition, dance, and spirit possession. Denominational affiliation is secondary to ritual in the black folk church. In essence, the type of ritual determines if a church is "folk" or not.

Before discussing the Easter Rock and the Rushin' religious rituals, it is important to define the parameters of the term ritual and how it is used in this study. In the words of Schultz and Lavenda (1998:355), "First, ritual is a repetitive social practice composed of a sequence of symbolic activities, in the form of dance, song, speech, bodily actions, and the manipulation of certain objects. . . . Second, it is set off from the social routines of everyday life. Third, rituals in any culture adhere to a characteristic, culturally-defined ritual schema. This means that members of a culture can tell that a certain sequence of activities is a ritual. . . . Finally, ritual action is closely connected to a specific set of ideas that are often encoded in myth. . . . The purpose for which a ritual is performed guides how these ideas are selected and symbolically enacted." Ritual events involve ways of embodying in action certain ideas that are important in society. Through the action, the ideas are reflected or transformed and some of these ideas are sanctified.

Edmund R. Leach informs us that "ritual action and belief are alike to be understood as forms of symbolic statements about the social order" (1954:14). To take an example from the African American context, during the Civil Rights movement when a crisis arose it was customary for blacks to gather at a black church to meet, pray, and sing before going out to face whatever adversity awaited them—a march, sit-in, boycott, or freedom ride on an interstate bus. To some people, these nonviolent responses also appeared passive. On closer inspection, we can see the prayer and singing ritual effectively release anxiety and tension, leaving the participants and leaders with better mental and emotional control. In addition, praying and singing together unites the community against the anticipated brutality. In this way, any subsequent pain and grief becomes communal and therefore less heavy on the individuals directly afflicted. What initially appears to be a passive reflex is in fact a courage-building ritual.

While there is no single or simple definition of ritual, it is clearly an essential part of all human societies. In examining the religious rituals of Easter Rock and Rushin', we need to bear in mind Leach's remark that "no interpretation of ritual sequences in man is possible unless the interpreter possesses detailed knowledge of the cultural matrix which provides the context for the rite in question" (1968).

Women in the black folk church exercise leadership and power through direct control of ceremonial and ritual events rather than through overt resistance to gender domination. James Scott's examination of the dynamics of power, resistance, and subordination suggest that the use of anonymity and ambiguity—gossip, folktales, songs, theater, and jokes—allow the powerless an ideological resistance to domination. He draws most of his evidence from slavery, serfdom, and caste subordination while also examining patriarchal domination, colonialism, and racism (1990:x).

Under the premise that structurally similar forms of domination will resemble each other, slavery and gender domination can be considered together, although slavery is more dramatically violent and gender domination more subtly imposed. Scott declares: "The ideologies justifying domination of this kind include formal assumptions about inferiority and superiority which, in turn, find expression in certain ritual or etiquette regulating public contact between strata" (1990:x–xi). Since I have acquired evidence from participants that the Easter Rock predates the Civil War era when the institution of slavery was still flourishing and there is evidence that the Rushin' tradition also originated during slavery in the Bahamas, I concur with Scott that "there is something useful to be said across cultures and historical epochs when our focus is narrowed by structural similarities" (1990:x). Diasporic sacred and circular rituals had similar performance structures and both were practiced during the institution of slavery. During this slave-master regime, the master dominated everybody—male and female—and everybody participated in the ritual whether it was open or clandestine. Postslavery, during emancipation and the Jim Crow era, gender domination takes the stage and the next subordinate group, the women in the church, organized the rituals that also provided them with outlets for leadership and power.

THE BAHAMIAN SETTING: YESTERDAY AND TODAY

Ninety five percent of Androsians are of African descent. They were imported as slaves—Ibo, Ijo, Yoruba, Mandingo, and Ashanti—and have the richest African cultural traditions in the Bahamas (Randolph 1994:243; Saunders 1994; Cash, Gordon, and Saunders 1991). In addition to the slaves, large groups of "liberated Africans" were transported to the Bahamas after being rescued by the British Royal Navy from Spanish ships. These ships were destined for Cuba and other Spanish colonies where Africans were to be enslaved. The British outlawed the slave trade in 1807 and interfered with the Spanish capture and transport of Africans. From 1811 to 1841, over 3,500 liberated Africans arrived on New Providence in Nassau and the majority was more than likely from Congo and Angola, the regions where the slave trade was concentrated during this era (Howard 2002:44). These people settled on Andros Island on the northeastern side—Mastic Point.

Following Britain's defeat in the American Revolutionary War, southern loyalists brought their slaves to the islands and grew cotton under the protection of the Crown. Bad times in neighboring North America often meant prosperity for the Bahamas. In 1861, during the American Civil War years, the Union Navy blockaded the islands in an attempt to cripple the Confederacy, and Bahamians grew rich running Confederate cotton to English mills and sending military equipment to Confederate rebels. By the end of the nineteenth century freed slaves found their way to Andros. Seminole Indians from Florida also came—first as visitors, then as settlers. The two groups intermarried and a small community sprang up around Red Bays where they worked in sponging and lumbering and farmed corn, harvested fish and plantains, yams, potatoes and peas (Grant 1821 cited in Howard 2002:47). One author noted in his journal entry while he was in this area that "Red Bay 'Indian people' did not associate much with the other blacks—Congo people—on the east side for a long time" (Goggin 1937:n.p.).

In 1964, Great Britain granted the islands self-government and in 1969 their status was changed from colony to Commonwealth. In 1973, the Commonwealth of the Bahamas became independent within the Commonwealth of Nations, but retained Queen Elizabeth II as constitutional head of state.

With the third largest barrier reef in the world on one side and the shallow water flats of the Great Bahama Bank on the other, Andros was overlooked as a tourist attraction and spared, for many years, from development. It is the largest island in the Bahamian archipelago and the least populated (Figure 1). Andros is also the fifth largest island in the circum-Caribbean region, following Cuba, Hispaniola, Jamaica, and Puerto Rico. Over the years, small communities have established themselves up and down the east coast of the island, with the population peaking at about ten thousand where it remains today.

BAHAMIAN RUSHIN'

When I returned to the Bahamas in 1996, I arrived on the island of Nassau a few days before Christmas in order to observe the secular Junkanoo rushing tradition again. After the Christmas festivities, we took our place on the main street in downtown Nassau—Bay Street. The Junkanoo celebration always follows Christmas on Boxing Day, December 26. On this day, the English planters designated a holiday for their enslaved Africans, who seized the opportunity to celebrate their brief period of freedom. Today, Junkanoo is celebrated on the day after Christmas and on New Year's Day. The year I was observing, it began around two o'clock in the morning, and Bay Street was full of people buzzing with excitement and great anticipation. To accommodate all the spectators, city officials lined Bay Street with bleachers and only certain officials and photographers with press passes

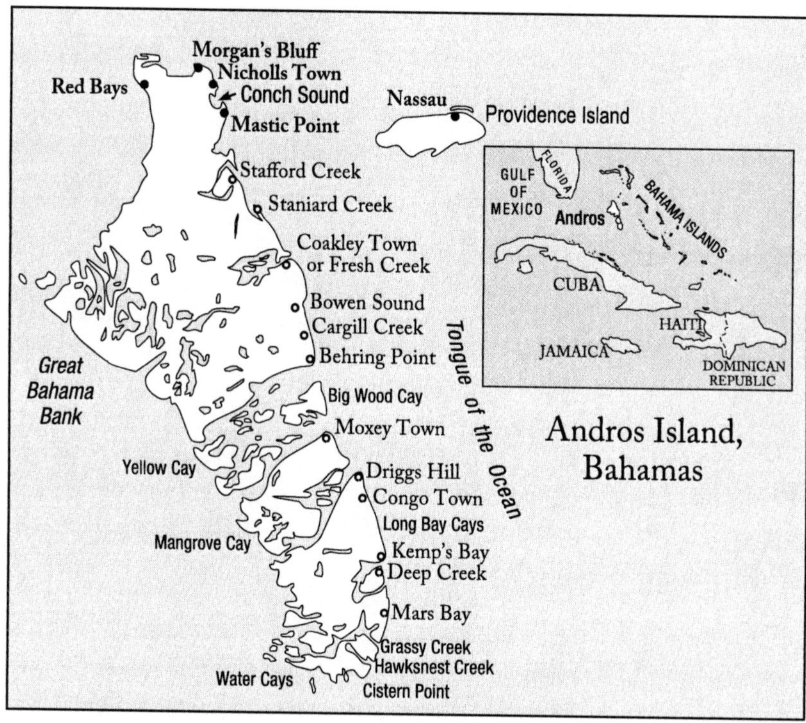

Figure 1. Map of Andros Island, Bahamas, with areas mentioned in the text in bold.

could stand near the parade and were able to dodge in and out to get close-up shots.

Arriving before the parade around one o'clock in the morning, I was able to observe the tuning of the goombay drums, which is sort of a ritual within itself. The drums are constructed from a wooden or metal barrel with a single membrane of sheep or goatskin stretched across the barrel and nailed over one end; the opposite end is left open. Many of the drummers from different groups assembled in an alley between buildings at one end of Bay Street and surrounded what appeared to be a large campfire. They stood and sat around the fire repairing and tuning drums using the heat from the fire. Some drummers actually attached sterno cans inside their drums so they could continue to heat the drum while they were participating in the long Junkanoo parade. The heat keeps the tonal pitch from fluctuating.

With the first sounds of the goombey drums off in the distance, I—with my camcorder—began looking for a space in the bleachers with the rest of the crowd. We were all anticipating the approaching spectacle of hundreds of junkanooers rushing down Bay Street. The music became louder and louder, like someone was gradually turning up the volume, until I could feel the pulsating beats within my entire body. Finally, the rival groups of masked dancers and drummers paraded before us, their colorful costumes a blur of multiple colors and shiny items rushing by. These groups vie for the glory, honor, and respect that comes from winning the Junkanoo parade. They perform specific themes with elaborately created costumes under the streetlights to the rhythm of drums, cowbells, whistles, and one-note horns that are blown very rhythmically. Each group is trying to be the best in originality of theme, beauty of costumes, selection and quality of music, and excellence in overall appearance and performance of the entire group. The parade goes around the route at least twice, depending on how long it is or how many groups are participating. This allows the judges and spectators to see each group at least twice. Later that morning after the sun has risen and competitors and parade viewers alike are exhausted, the winner is announced. For many, this will be the Junkanoo topic for months to come, and for others, for the remainder of the year. What was the "edge" the winner had to win the title? Will the winner retain the title next year? What will other groups have to do to surpass the winner? These questions and other can only be answered in the next year's anticipated competition.

Along with noticing the varying sizes of cowbells (flat-sided clapper bells ranging in size from six to fourteen inches) and whistles, I was also more conscious of the body and feet movements. The traditional movement is a basic slide step in which the right foot slides up and the right hip goes down, the left hip goes up and out simultaneously. This is the exact movement used in the sacred Rushin' ritual and it is the performance practice that connects one ritual to the other.

After the secular rushin' experience, it was time to move on to the sacred. The next day, we boarded a small commuter plane to Andros Island, which is about a twenty-five-minute flight from Nassau. While waiting in the airport in Nassau, I was able to speak to most of the people. There were only two tourists on board. All the other people were residents of Andros Island returning home from visiting relatives and friends for Christmas and/or Junkanoo festivities and residents of Nassau going to visit relatives and friends on Andros Island for the New Year's festivities.

Moving from Nassau, the main tourist island in the Bahamas, to Andros, the main family island in the Bahamas, was almost akin to moving from daylight to dark. Although there are secluded and quiet beaches on Nassau, Andros has miles of secluded and unspoiled quiet beaches and quiet communities. However the small settlement of Conch Sound comes alive at Christmas, New Year's, and Easter as people come from neighboring communities to the Church of God of Prophecy, where the unique expression of praise called Rushin' is held. Mother Pratt, the minister of the church states: "Other settlements stopped doing it, but we find it very appropriate here in Conch Sound and we have our reason and purpose for it. We want to keep the thing as sacred unto God, we don't rush as a part of Junkanoo or some fun thing, it's a piece of pleasure yes, but we make sure we do it seriously . . . and we keeps it under subjection. When there's going to be a rushin' after service, I myself, being pastor, would stand and let the people know, 'now its time to worship God in another way'" (1996). The "other way" of worshipping that Mother Pratt is referring to is their version of the "ring shout." A reference to ring dances in the Bahamas was made in E. Clement Bethel's work. He states: "In The Bahamas alone, we need look no further than the Bahamian ring dances—the Fire Dance and the Jumping Dance—for examples of rituals which were routinely hidden from masters. The New World Africans were painfully aware of their vulnerability. Consequently, they allowed their masters no hold on the source of their inner strength—religion, sorcery, herbal lore, the knowledge of the true names of things. What they considered most powerful was what they most perfectly concealed" (1991:12). Bethel does not discuss these dances further, but it is likely that the ring dances were concealed until after emancipation. Then they began to do them openly, but only after the regular worship service was over.

According to Mother Pratt and my observations in 1996, the church service was similar to their regular service except for the extra musical performances and the fact that the minister gave a talk, which was not like the regular sermon. They started with a devotional period that included biblical scripture reading, prayer, chanted response to prayer, a choir selection, and a welcome for all guests. There were soloists and guest groups from other churches performing along with their usual church choir performances. In addition, the church house band accompanied the choir and anybody else who wanted to be accompanied. The leader of the band and two other members were Mother Pratt's sons. During the service a collection was taken and a prayer of thanks was given for the funds collected, then the program resumed. After more hymn singing and gospel music between testimonials and short sermonettes, the minister "opened the doors of the church." In essence, she asked for the sinners, backsliders, and those that only needed a "church home" to come and join or be a member of the church. A few people came to the front of the pulpit while the singing continued and after the congregation stopped singing, the secretary of the church stated the names and desires of the people that came forth. Next, Mother Pratt made the announcement to remind visitors and friends about the sacred Rushin' that was to take place in the Fellowship Hall (the former main church) immediately following the New Year's Eve service. Afterwards, she gave the benediction and the service ended with everyone shaking hands or hugging.

Those that wanted to participate in the Rushin' moved next door to the Fellowship Hall. This building had a wooden floor and movable chairs. Since the church service was held at night, during the day women had moved the chairs close to the walls of the Hall. The women placed a table on the outside of the circle, near the former pulpit space, to hold donations (Figure 2). As members of the congregation moved around the church in

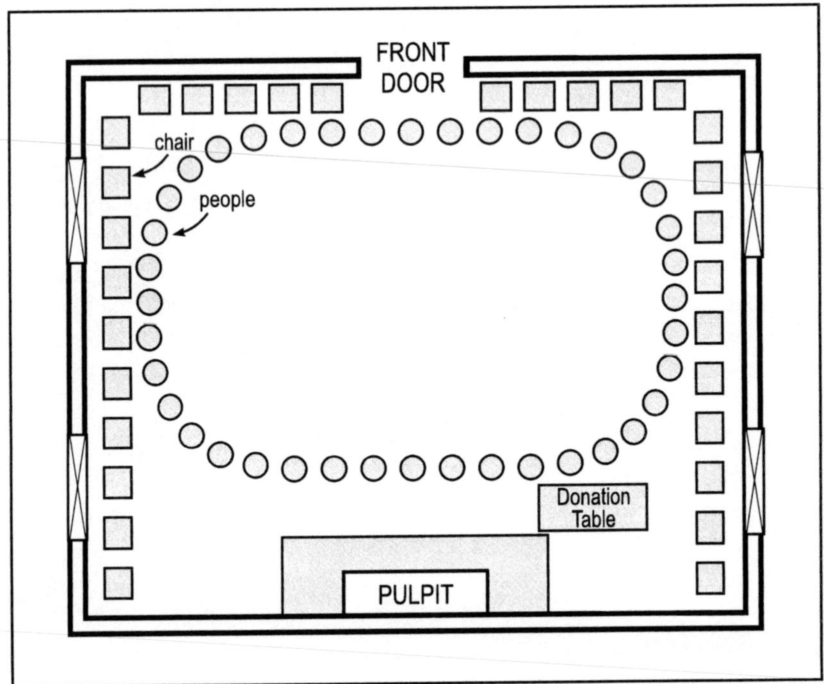

Figure 2. Church diagram of sacred Rushing, Church of God of Prophecy Fellowship Hall, Conch Sound, Andros Island, Bahamas.

Figure 3. Rushing ritual, Church of God of Prophecy Fellowship Hall, Conch Sound, Andros Island, Bahamas. J. Nash Porter, photographer, © 1996.

the circle, they placed money on the table. These donations were to be used for the youth fund in the church.

The rush began as the ritual performers, who are members of the congregation, began to sing the old spirituals and hymns that had been arranged as gospel songs. A band consisting of bass and rhythm guitars, a drumset, and a trumpet accompanied them. Traditionally, "rhyming songs" would have been performed *a capella* by all (Saunders 1995).[1] In my own examination of the ritual in 1996, the performers moved in a counterclockwise circle dance, at times clapping their hands (Figure 3). Congregants waited on the sideline for their chance to rush around the church because a large number of male and female members and nonmembers participated in the Rushin'. Later in the night as more people came to participate, double lines formed.

Before the event, older women of the church prepared food like fried chicken, fish and conch fritters, and plantains. Soft drinks, water, and coffee were brought to the kitchen, which was in a separate building behind the church. This food was prepared to be sold to participants throughout the night because the Rushin' usually lasts until "day clean," meaning sunrise.

THE LOUISIANA SETTING: YESTERDAY AND TODAY

The rich alluvial plain encompassing a large portion of the northeastern region of Louisiana, referred to as the Delta, is the state's Cotton Belt. According to the WPA history, many Anglos who moved to Franklin Parish and subsequently to Winnsboro in 1843 came from somewhere else, bringing their slaves with them (Oliver and Murphy 1973). Franklin Parish had fewer slaves (Figure 4) because it was not one of the wealthy cotton growing parishes fronting the Mississippi River. Its settlers were mainly Anglo-Saxon and Scotch-Irish. Until 1859, when the first steam gin was built, horsepower operated cotton gins, limiting output to only four or five bales a day. However, the city of Natchez, across the Mississippi River, had large slave markets prior to the Civil War and large numbers of descendents of enslaved Africans brought to Louisiana from the Atlantic coast can be found in the Delta (Oliver and Murphy 1937).

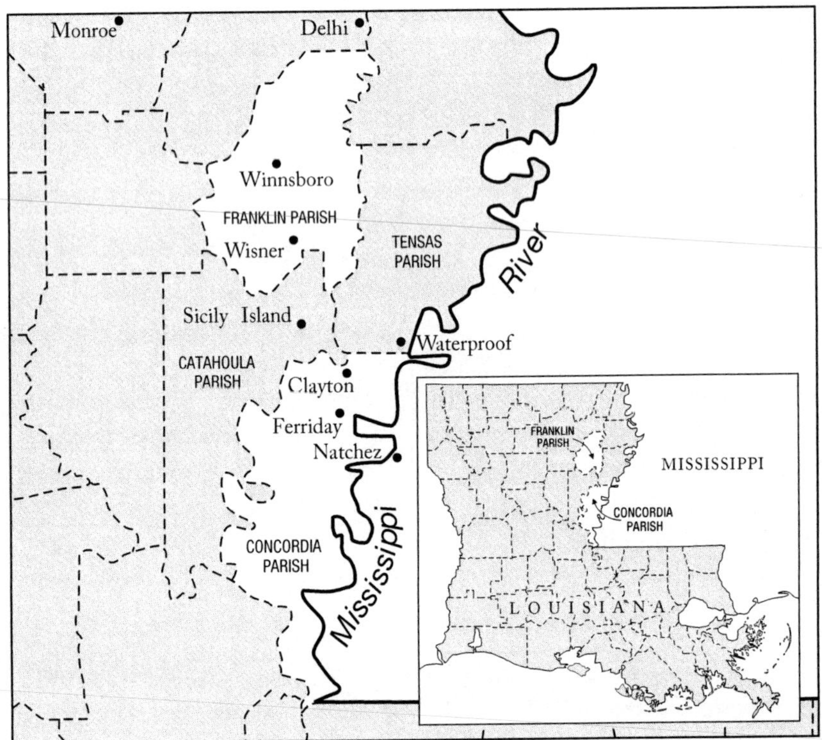

Figure 4. Map of Louisiana parishes indicating the towns where at least one church held the Easter Rock ritual.

The Village of Winnsboro became the parish seat in 1845 and the area survived the Civil War to see growth and expansion with the coming of the railroad in 1890. The New Orleans and the North Western Railroad connected the parish from north to south and Governor William Wright Heard issued a proclamation declaring the Village of Winnsboro incorporated in 1902 (Oliver and Murphy 1937). Today, the town of Winnsboro is located on Louisiana Highway 15, thirty-seven miles from Monroe, Louisiana, and fifty-five miles from Natchez, Mississippi.

LOUISIANA ROCKIN'

Although the following ethnography is representative of many years of participant observations, audio- and videotaping, and field notes, most of the data is taken from my field notes and videotapes from the 1999 Easter Rock ritual. A few days before the ceremony at The Original True Light Baptist Church in Winnsboro, I visited the homes of several participants and spoke with them as they prepared for the annual celebration. The women who performed the ritual required several days of preparation before Easter eve. The preparations included dressmaking and repairing, cake baking, and refurbishing the banner. I also visited the church the day before the ritual because the coordinator of the Easter Rock, Ms. Haddie Addison and a few of the other women "rockers" had to rearrange the pews against the walls, give the church its Easter cleaning, and decorate it with pastel crepe paper streamers. They also brought young adults with them to help clean the church and to teach them what to do to prepare for the actual ritual.

On the day of the ritual people began to gather outside of the church, visiting with each other while a few women made last-minute preparations inside the church. I entered the church and took a seat in one of the pews that had been pushed against the sides of the sanctuary, leaving a wide area in the middle of the floor for the rocking circle. Two long tables positioned in the middle of the floor were draped in white cloth with pastel crepe-paper streamers. The windows, the door entrances, and the pulpit of the church all were adorned with streamers as well.

The ceremony began when the mistress of ceremony took her place at the dais on the floor beside the elevated pulpit. Although a woman directed the ritual, she did not do so from the pulpit. Even during this female-driven event, the male minister was still the only one in the pulpit. The mistress of ceremony led the congregation in a typical devotion and worship service.

An elderly male deacon initiated the call to worship from the dais, performed an opening prayer, and led the congregation in a lined-out hymn.[2] Reverend J. L. McDowell gave the greetings from the pulpit and a female visitor from another church gave the acceptance from the dais. Someone sang a solo and another person gave the occasion. Several congregation members and visitors from other churches performed very spiritual and emotional solos and some elderly women shouted, displaying a physical show of emotions while "filled with the Holy Spirit." One seated member, for example, threw both arms in the air and shouted, "Thank you Jesus!" When emotions died down, a deacon or another elderly person started another lined-out hymn. Some of these practices are common in the devotional segment of a regular church service. However in the devotional setting they are preparing the congregants for the minister's sermon; in this setting, they are preparing them for the Easter Rock, the annual celebration of the risen Christ. After the deacon and the congregation sang two verses, a third verse began and the lights were turned off. These lined-out hymns and turning out the lights were the cues for the Rock to begin.

A walking procession of twelve women started from the back of the sanctuary, moving toward the center to encircle the table. In the earlier days these women were the elderly "mothers of the church" and were purported to be members of the benevolent society (Pollard 1997; Gregory 1962).[3] As they proceeded in a counterclockwise direction around the table, the rockers began to sing "When the Saints Go Marching In" in a dirgelike style, and the surrounding congregation augmented the singing. The entire ceremony was done *a capella* with only handclapping and foot stamping to accompany the songs. Eleven of the women in the procession followed each other around the table carrying burning kerosene lamps, and the leader (the twelfth woman) carried a symbolic representation of the cross, a circular banner with streamers flowing from it.

After circling several times, the women placed the lamps on the table in a straight line. They then repeated these actions to place the twelve cakes on the table (Figure 5). Traditionally, all the cakes were layered with white icing and they were made by only two or three people. Today, however, there is a mixture of colors and types of cakes—pound, chocolate, layered with jelly filling, layered with coconut filling, angel food—because more people contribute cakes and while some are home baked, others are purchased from the store or bakery. Ms. Addison noted that "People don't bake cakes like they used to, so we can't be choicey. We have to be thankful for what we get" (1999).

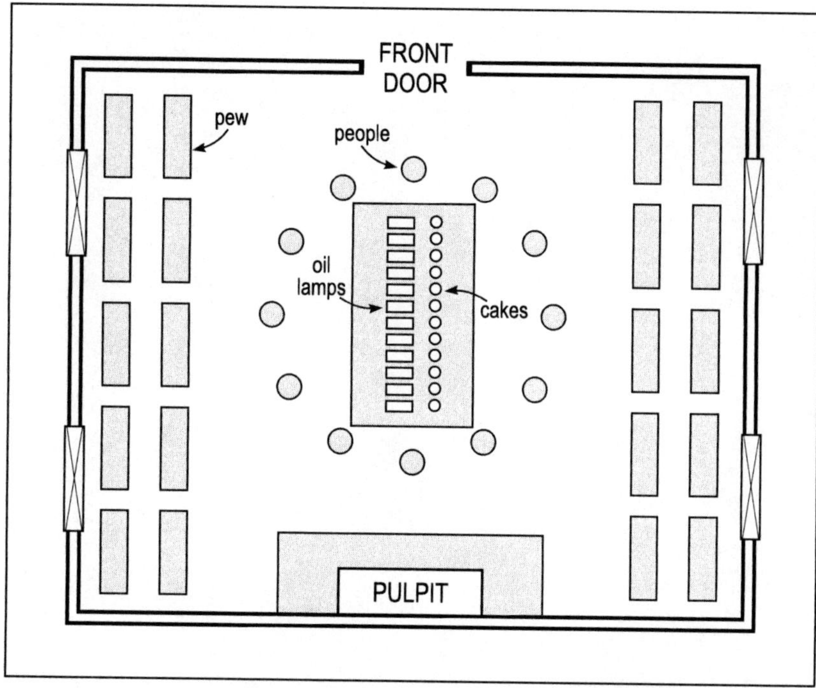

Figure 5. Church diagram of Easter Rock, True Light Baptist Church, Winnsboro, Louisiana.

Still singing "When the Saints Go Marching In" and without missing a step, the women proceeded around the table while someone passed the cakes to them through the door in the back of the church. They slowly placed the twelve cakes on the table as they marched around it. The rockers made a few more rounds after the cakes were placed, and then the tempo accelerated, the song changed, and the steps of the rockers quickened and changed.

At this key moment, the rockers were transitioning into the second and heightened phase of the Rock. They began to sing "Oh David," an old up-tempo shout or rock song that is no longer performed except for this ritual. This faster song was more like a chant, and the rockers began to move more quickly, performing the distinctive rocking step that gives this ritual its name (Figure 6). The step constitutes a step-slide and skip from one side to the other, and some participants perform it without taking their feet off the floor. This phase of the Rock can continue for several hours or well into the next morning with practitioners alternating between sitting and rocking.

Figure 6. Easter Rock ritual, True Light Baptist Church, Winnsboro, La. J. Nash Porter, photographer, © 1999.

(In an older time, according to practitioners I interviewed, the ritual continued until the "sun shouted," or dawn; in 1999, the ritual ended at about ten o'clock at night.) This second phase is highly charged with emotion, and some of the rockers and congregants "caught the Spirit" by either shouting or going into trance. The repetitive rhythm of the congregants dancing feet has the driving percussive texture of the African drum. In the Rock, as in many African-derived sacred rituals, the repetitive beaten rhythms from the drum or from feet on the hard floor tend to cause some participants to shout, go into trance, or invoke the Spirit. The night I was observing, the chant "Oh David" was changed after some time to the spiritual "Elijah Rock" without missing a beat. Whether the group sings the same song or switches songs depends on who is leading the song and sometimes who is carrying the banner at the time. However, this does not mean that the banner carrier always leads and determines the song.

How long the rockers circle seems to depend on the movement of the spirit or the degree of fatigue. When The Original True Light rockers were tired, they ceased rocking for a while before resuming the program. At this transition, the mistress of ceremony announced that it was time for the congregation to "honor God by giving," that is, time for the collection. The mistress of ceremony volunteered two members to collect the offering from the other participants, who marched around the church and gave their offering while singing a congregational hymn. A deacon prayed over the funds in the collection plate. Announcements were made and guest singers from different churches performed a few solos; some singers were even requested to sing certain songs. These songsters were well known by members of the congregation for having one or two "signature songs."[4] After the soloists performed, the deacon once again began a long-meter hymn with the congregation; after singing a while, they turned off the lights, which signaled that the Rock was beginning again.

The rockers again fell in line and began to rock around the table for this second phase of the ritual. The line began like the first one, with the banner carrier in front. This time, the participants rocked for an interval, singing the same songs, but then the mistress of ceremony invited other members of the congregation and guests to join in the Rock. For at least the last decade, the ritual has usually ended between nine thirty and ten o'clock. After the program and ritual ended, the coordinator "gave words of thanks" and everybody was invited for the repast or refreshments, which consisted of the twelve ritual cakes and red fruit punch. During earlier years when the Rock lasted all night, the women brought more substantial food, like fried chicken and potato salad, to actually feed people during the night. The ceremony would last until it was time to go to Easter Sunrise service.

MAY THE CIRCLE BE UNBROKEN

Unlike the Andros Island Rushin' ceremonies, which take place on Christmas, New Years, and Easter, the north Louisiana Rocking ceremony currently takes place only on Easter eve. However, in earlier days, Rocks in Concordia Parish were not exclusively for Easter. There are some accounts by the elders of Rocks such as the Ship of Zion ceremony held on New Year's Eve. Sturman mentions the Ship of Zion ceremony in her work, but she does not discuss it further and the participants in Winnsboro are not familiar with this tradition. In addition, Easter Rocks were held in Clayton and some were held in November and referred to as the Harvest Rock ceremony (Sturman 1994:28). There have also been accounts of another Delta congregation that sponsored Rocks on a weekly basis to attract youth to the church and to keep them out of trouble (Sturman 1994:28). Today, in Winnsboro, Louisiana, the participants claim that the Rock is relegated solely to Easter.

From the participant accounts on Andros Island, it appears that unlike the Rock in Louisiana, the Rushin' ceremony does not have an abundance of symbolic meaning and pageantry pertaining to the birth or passion of Christ. However, it is possible that there was more spirituality, pageantry, and symbolism that now has passed from the historical memory of the elderly practitioners.

Various elders who had actively participated for many years in the Rock in Winnsboro gave me their interpretations of its symbolism as well as information their older relatives passed on to them. This information has been transmitted through several generations, so some of the symbolic representations have taken on multiple meanings, depending on who is giving an account of the ritual. For example in some ceremonies the twelve women moving around the table represent and are referred to as the twelve saints, while others refer to them as the twelve disciples of Christ. The cakes represent the twelve tribes of Israel and the unleavened bread at the Last Supper. Easter eggs are placed on the table, according to the elders, to symbolize new birth and the stone that was rolled away from the tomb of Christ on Easter Sunday morning.

There is a predominance of the color white, which represents purity: the twelve women who first proceed around the circle are wearing white dresses, the tables are draped in white cloths, in previous times all cakes had white icing, and the base of the banner is white. The red fruit punch that is served to congregants after the Rock represents the blood of Jesus Christ. Several participants recalled that homemade wine was used in earlier days (Bowie 1995). The round banner on the staff and the person carrying it symbolize Christ carrying the cross. The banner puller who processes behind the banner carrier and pulls rhythmically on the two streamers or light ropes connected to the banner, symbolizes Simon the Cyrenian who helped Jesus bear the cross on his way to Golgotha.[5]

The banner itself warrants more analysis, as it is apparently a circular representation of the cross. Why have participants used a circle mounted on top of a staff to represent the cross when they could have easily made a wooden cross? I posed this question to each elderly person in the community who I interviewed. Invariably, I was told about the ways the banner has changed over the years from basic white slipcovers to a white banner with colored streamers flowing. However, no one ventured to speculate about the significance of the circled cross or its origins, except to note that "it has always been that way" and "it is the tradition."

Since both rituals are pre–Civil War and it is obvious that they both have antecedents in West Africa, I suggest that the Easter Rock circular cross icon as well as the counterclockwise circular dance were maintained by enslaved Africans on plantations in Franklin and Concordia Parishes. I suggest the same for the enslaved and liberated Africans on the northeast section of Andros Island. There are many complexities involved in determining Kongo influences in the diaspora, specifically Louisiana and the Bahamas. Although it is not my intention in this study to engage in a lengthy discussion on possible origins and African retentions, I will make a few brief observations.

African influences emerge in the diaspora in many places and in many ways. Examples include music, vernacular English, metaphysical traditions of healing with herbs and roots, philosophic and visual traditions, dance and spirituality. The power of cultural memory is most readily discernible in spirituality in the diaspora. The Atlantic slave trade reflects the expansion of European slave trafficking into the heart of Yoruba, Angola and Kongo societies during the seventeenth, eighteenth, and nineteenth centuries. Thousands of Africans were abducted from this culturally rich area and they continued to foster their heritage in the Western Hemisphere. In Haiti it was Vodun, in Brazil, Condomble, in Cuba it was Santería, and in the Bahamas and the United States, it was Afro-Protestant based religions such as Baptist and Methodist accompanied by the ever-present ring-shout after the regular service.

Before the Civil War, ring-shouts were ubiquitous throughout the plantation South, especially in Virginia, Alabama, and Georgia (Sobel 1979:140–42). The ring-shout obviously continued as an African American religious ritual form after emancipation. In 1934 folklorists John and Alan Lomax observed ring shouts in Louisiana, Texas, and Georgia, as well as in the Bahamas, where many enslaved Africans and Sea Islanders were taken as slaves of owners loyal to the British cause during the American Revolutionary War (Raboteau 1978:70). Enslaved and liberated Africans from the Kongo were brought to Louisiana and Andros Islands in the 1700s and 1800s. For instance, in her work focusing on the Point Coupee revolt during the Spanish rule, Gwendolyn Hall (1992) writes that a slave ship, the La Poloma, was recorded in Point Coupee bringing slaves probably to replace those exiled or executed after the 1795 revolt. All of the slaves on board were Kongolese (1992:280). Other enslaved Africans from the Kongo were brought into Louisiana during the Haitian Revolution (Geggus 1989:23).

It is generally accepted that at the time of emancipation, slaves were still overwhelmingly African in culture. Sterling Stuckey, a leading historian, has explored the folklore of American slaves by examining it through a cross-cultural, Pan-African lens. In Stuckey's seminal work, *Slave Culture* (1987), he establishes what he refers to as the "black ethos in slavery." Essentially, he substantiates the centrality of an African ancestral ritual—the circle dance—to the black religious and artistic experience. He writes:

> The majority of Africans brought to North America to be enslaved were from the central and western areas of Africa—from Congo-Angola, Nigeria, Dahomey, Togo, the Gold Coast, and Sierra Leone. In these areas, an integral part of religion and culture was movement in a ring during ceremonies honoring the ancestors. There is, in fact, substantial evidence for the importance of the ancestral function of the circle in West Africa, but the circle ritual imported by Africans from the Congo region was so powerful in this elaboration of a religious vision that it contributed disproportionately to the centrality of the circle in slavery. The use of the circle for religious purposes in slavery was so consistent and profound that one could argue that it was what gave form and meaning to black religion and art. (Stuckey 1987:10–11)

Circular dances are also linked to the burial ceremony, which is the most important of all African rituals. According to art historian Robert F. Thompson, in Bakongo burial ceremonies, mourners moved around the body of the deceased in a counterclockwise direction with their feet imprinting a circle on the earth (Thompson 1981:54, 28). I recently (2004) observed three funerals in the coastal region of Ghana in Woe between Keta and Anloga, all of which included some form of circular dancing or processing in relationship to the deceased body. The funeral of a 108-year-old man was dense with circular movements of individuals, groups, and individuals with animal sacrifices, all moving around the deceased in a counterclockwise direction.

The Easter Rock counterclockwise circular dance could also be symbolically linked to burial as interpreted through Christian doctrine of the ritual burial of Jesus Christ after his crucifixion. The Easter Rock ritual is a condensed celebration of the last three days of Christ on earth: the crucifixion, burial, and resurrection. Because of the temperate regional climate, Easter is also the time in many southern rural Baptist churches when baptisms are held in the river, lake, or creek. The candidate is symbolically buried under water in Christ, where sins are washed away, and he/she is raised up to walk in the newness of life.

Furthermore, the circular cross and staff symbolize a movement from one state of being in the Kongo religious system to a higher one. The circular cross is also the sign of the four moments of the sun, which is the Kongo emblem of spiritual continuity and renaissance (Thompson 1981:54, 28). Therefore, the circular banner that represents the cross in the Easter Rock may be the same symbol that represents the theme of the circular dance—dying to begin again and consequently maintaining the continuous flow of life. Christianity provided a protective exterior to cover the more complex sacred African practices and principles that were operative. Again, there are many complexities involved in making these interpretations, and it obviously requires more research, thought, and discussion.

ROCKIN' AND RUSHIN' TO THE BEAT

In 1996 when I walked into the Church of God of Prophecy Fellowship Hall in Conch Sound, I was truly disappointed. When I observed the band members setting up their instruments and sound system on the stage, which was once the pulpit, I knew that I would not be hearing the traditional rushing music. People began congregating and talking in the Hall, some were standing and others sitting in the chairs around the wall, but all were anticipating a night of rushing. After everything was set on the stage, the leader of the band welcomed everybody, said a few words, and the band began to play very loud. The repertoire was a combination of "gospelized spirituals and hymns," traditional songs with accompanied modern arrangements. Some of the songs were "This Lil' Light of Mine," "I'll Fly Away," "Sweet Home," and "What a Friend We Have in Jesus." Because there was an abundance of youth in the church and because Mother Pratt, the minister, had several sons who were musicians, the traditional Rushin' had made a modern transition.

Since a rural black church without youth is by definition nearly dead, its life is determined to a substantial degree by its ability to attract, hold, and service a constituency of young people. Church officials have attempted to fill the gap and maintain the youth membership by not only instituting new programs and youth ministries, but also by examining new trends in music. Music is so important in the Black Church as a monolithic institution that it is a primary means of attracting members and sustaining spiritual growth. The old traditional songs do not fare well against contemporary songs or arrangements.

Nevertheless, some of the elders in the Conch Sound community gave me a sense of the music of the earlier rushin' tradition, before the youth of the church transformed the music into its modern gospelized version. I interviewed Mr. Rudolph Saunders, who was born in 1902 and could remember rushin' since he was a boy of ten years living in Mastic Point. He was ninety-five years old at the time of our interview. He related many vivid descriptions of rushin' rituals growing up on Andros Island. Because I was so eager to hear what the songs sounded like when he was still participating in the Rush, I gently encouraged him to sing one for me. He said, "my wife, she used to rhyme the anthem for the people to rush, but not me 'cause I ain't got good voice." After making excuses for his bad voice, he reluctantly consented:

> Stoop down to the livin' water, stoop down to the livin' water.
> Stoop down to the livin' water, stoop down and drink and live.
>
> Sinner knock, knock to my door, sinner knock to my door last night.
> Sinner knock, knock to my door, sinner knock to my door last night
>
> I'm goin' down to the Jordan River, sinner knock to my door last night.
> I'm goin' down to the Jordan River, sinner knock to my door last night.
>
> Jordan River so chilly and cold, sinner knock to my door last night.
> Chilly and cold 'til it ache my soul, sinner knock to my door last night.

Predictably, escape themes and motives appear again and again in African American folk spirituals. Then there are the ubiquitous allusions to water—

specifically to the Jordan River, stream, or banks—and to boats or ships that sail on water—particularly the Ship of Zion. This song ties into the slave institution in the Bahamas. What Mr. Saunders sang was an example of a "rhyming spiritual," which is the distinctive Bahamian type of sacred song. In this instance, "rhyming" does not refer to a requirement that the final syllables rhyme, although they sometimes do. In this context, rhyming means verse, which involves intoning couplets against a melodic background of voices (Stecher and Siegel 1998).

It is uncanny how close the rhyming songs sound to the African American folk spiritual; the similarities are striking in terms of texts, melodies and performance practices. There is a logical explanation. The rhyming songs and their performance style are the result of alternate periods of contact with and isolation from the U.S. mainland. During the American Revolution, a group of loyalists left the Carolinas and Georgia with their enslaved Africans and settled in Abaco Cays in the Bahamas. It was there that an enclave of free black people had also come to live around 1776 (Howard 2002:44, 62). During this period spirituals were developing in the southern plantation area and it is very likely that the enslaved as well as the free blacks brought their songs with them.

Emancipation came to the Caribbean much sooner than it did to the mainland. For the Bahamas, it occurred in 1838. In the southern United States, enslaved blacks and Seminole Indians escaped and sought refuge in the free islands. Andros was particularly suitable because of its vast size, undeveloped land, and isolation from the other islands. Until the end of the Civil War (1865), there was a continuous inflow of African Americans to Andros, and of course they brought their songs. Many of their songs were adapted to the text, style, and performance practice of the African American folk spirituals. Many of the texts were taken from biblical scripture and the tradition of "singing sermons," while others pertained to secular life on the island, specifically, work songs (Stecher and Siegel 1998:n.p.; Bethel 1978:87).

The Easter Rock songs are traditionally a combination of the African American version of the lined-out or long-meter hymns and the folk spirituals and chants used specifically for shouts or in this case rocks. By all indications from the elderly participants, the Easter Rock is a pre–Civil War ritual and it is highly possible that the chants originated during this time or were later influenced by pre–Civil War spirituals. James Weldon Johnson writing in 1925 explains:

> Brief mention must be made of another class of Negro songs. This is a remnant of songs allied to the Spirituals but which cannot be strictly classified with them. They are the "shout songs." These songs are not true spirituals. . . . This term "shout songs" has no reference to the loud, jubilant Spirituals, which are often so termed by writers on Negro music; it has reference to the songs or, better, the chants used to accompany the "ring shout." The "ring shout," in truth, is nothing more or less than the survival of a primitive African dance, which in quite an understandable way attached itself in the early days to the Negro's Christian worship. (Johnson and Johnson 1969:32–33)

The spirituals and chants were built on the form so common to West African songs, a leading call and response. They also shared many points of stylistic similarity: overlapping of leader and chorus, extended repetition of short melodic phrases, *a capella*, layered rhythms, improvisation of text and melody, percussive emphasis, and bodily movement. According to elderly participants and published sources, in earlier years there was a larger selection of the actual rock chants, but now fewer are sung and rocked to at the Winnsboro Easter Rock (Seale and Seale 1942; Oster 1958; Sturman 1993). In this setting, "Oh David" is the perennial favorite for the actual rock. When I asked Mrs. Jimmie Lee Jones (personal interview 1996) why this song-chant was the favorite, she replied:

> They used David, because David was a warrior and David was a winner and Christ was a winner for our souls. They would symbolize David going out to the King and finding out that the King was afraid of the Philistines. David asked them, "Now, what's the matter now" and they said they feared the Philistines. So, David was just a boy and so he told them that he would go out. And so that is when you hear the song say, "Where you going little boy out on the field?" He was a boy taking a man's job going out to fight Goliath. And Goliath made fun of him saying, "and you send just a lad." There are so many things in this song.
>
> Leader: Tell me what's the matter now?
> Chorus: Oh David.
> Leader: Tell me what's the matter now?
> Chorus: Oh David.
> Leader: Oh what did Goliath say?
> Chorus: Oh David.
> Leader: Oh what did Goliath say?
> Chorus: Oh David.
> Leader: Lord, I'm in trouble now.

Chorus: Oh David.
Leader: Lord, I'm in trouble now.
Chorus: Oh David.
Leader: Send me a man right now.
Chorus: Oh David.
Leader: Send me a upright man.
Chorus: Oh David
Leader: A man that's fit for war.
Chorus: Oh David.
Leader: A man not afraid to die.
Chorus: Oh David.
Leader: Tell me where you goin' lil' boy?
Chorus: Oh David.
Leader: Tell me where you goin' lil' boy?
Chorus: Oh David
Leader: Goin' out on that field.
Chorus: Oh David
Leader: Goin' out on that field.
Chorus: Oh David.
Leader: Lor—dey, Lor—dey.
Leader: Lord I'm in trouble now.
Chorus: Oh David.
Leader: I believe I'll say my prayers.

Mrs. Jones continues,

> David played a harp, he played a hundred strings. David played this and kept the evil spirits off of Saul after Saul had sinned and so we sing:
>
> Leader: Play on your hundred strings. [repeat]
> Chorus: Oh David.
> Leader: Play like you did for Saul, oh David. [repeat]
> Chorus: Oh David.

Mrs. Jones adds,

> We never sing this song for anything else. This song was made from Bible. You can go with the rhythm and it is not slow. You can hear the rhythms with your hands [clapping] and feet as they go around.

It is generally understood that many of the African American folk spirituals, created during the antebellum era, have double meanings. These songs were used to circumvent certain restrictions by communicating coded messages. Even though the Easter Rock ritual is commemorating the resurrection of Christ, the song-chant "Oh David" is deemed suitable for the occasion. In essence, enslaved blacks had an Old Testament bias. Among their revered heroes about whom they sang constantly were Moses, Daniel, Jonah, Gabriel, and David. All the themes were conceptually dealing with good against bad, the weaker conquering the stronger, and the enslaved conquering the slave master. Therefore, it was significant to the enslaved that little David triumphed over the great Goliath with a stone, since the enslaved had no weapons. David was a favorite scriptural hero of the enslaved Africans—judging by the number of times they sang about him in sacred folksongs. Of course they put in drama and excitement while reshaping the original story to their own concerns. This type of theme can be anticipated, for it is a theme of any oppressed people who are determined to "overcome" and it is another form of hidden transcript.

HIDDEN TRANSCRIPTS

The similarity of the story of David and Goliath with the plight of blacks in bondage is all too clear. In this respect there was a latent and symbolic element of protest in the enslaved black's religious song—spirituals and chants. Similarly, "Astute slave holders undoubtedly realized that the attention of Joshua and Moses in the slave Christianity had something to do with their prophetic roles as liberators of the Israelites from bondage. But since they were, after all, Old Testament prophets, slaves could hardly be punished for revering them as part of their—authorized—Christian faith" (Scott 1990:158). There are many published sources examining double meaning and historical parallels to Biblical bondage in African American spiritual music (Boykin 1947; Brown 1941; Dawson 1955; Johnson and Johnson 1925; Levine 1972; and Lovell 1972).

Even though the women had full authority to change whatever they wanted to change in the Easter Rock, they maintained the chant "Oh David" because it was considered to be a hidden transcript that served other purposes. The good David not only triumphed over bad Goliath, but he went on to eventually become a righteous king. Many of the slave folksongs had an inevitable sadness, as W. E. B. DuBois's essay, "Sorrow Songs," in the *Souls of Black Folk* (1903), so eloquently reminds us. However, many more were characterized by confidence than by despair. There was confidence that contemporary power relationships were not immutable.

Examining the commonalities of the Rockin' and the Rushin' rituals, I have observed that 1) they are not a part of the regular church worship service, 2) that their traditional choice of music is very similar, and 3) that they both are organized, directed, and maintained by women.

In the case of the Easter Rock, the women do everything. They bake the cakes, mend and/or construct the white dresses, purchase the oil for the lamps, boil and color the Easter eggs or purchase candy eggs, spring clean and decorate the church, prepare the children, mend or construct the banner, develop programs, and contact and invite potential participants for the program. During my visits, one woman, Ms. Haddie Addison, orchestrated the entire event. If someone did not perform her delegated task, in Ms. Addison's words, she had to "take up the slack." Ms. Addison has been the guiding force for many years after she "inherited" the Rock from her mother when she decided she was getting too old for the complex responsibility of orchestrating all those tasks.

In Conch Sound on Andros Island, Mother Pratt was the guiding force for the Rush and the minister of the church. It is significant to note here that her church, the only one on the island ministered by a woman, was also the only one on the island that consistently maintained the Rushin' tradition. Since she is the minister, she is no longer directly involved in the Rush; the women of the church orchestrate and implement all the tasks. Since this ritual does not incorporate or involve symbolic preparation and biblical symbolic icons as the Easter Rock, there is not as much preparation. However, the women cleaned the church, rearranged the chairs, set up the money table, purchased the food and drinks and did all the cooking. The food was prepared and cooked on the night of the Rush. When people tired of Rushin' and wanted something to eat and drink, they went to the "out-kitchen," a small separate building set apart from the church, and purchased food, sodas or coffee. The money that was collected for the food and in the Rushin' was used for the Youth Fund.

In my observations and from accounts of elderly participants, neither ritual is ever incorporated into a regular church service, they are always performed at night, and they are community events and not just for one congregation. The creativity of these women chanters and rockers has carried their community's heritage over many decades and historical transitions. As the preservers of music and ritual, these women also preserve their authority and power within the church and the community. In these roles, they remain within their cultural parameters while simultaneously engaging hidden transcripts.

In the transition from West and Central Africa to the diaspora, the importance of the religious role of women was maintained most clearly in the Afro-Caribbean and Afro-Latin religious traditions where the survival of African religious influences were strongest. In all of the African-based diaspora religions, women maintained their roles as priestesses. In the United States and the Bahamas where Protestant Christianity dominated, the African religious influences took an indirect and sublimated form, and we can still examine these forms in smaller and more rural congregations. The women who have strong roles in these churches have positions as cultural preservers rather than positions that are instrumental, political, or economical.

In examining the Louisiana Easter Rock and the Bahamian Rushin' traditions I have focused on a description of the traditions, the role of the women in each, the music, and other symbolic factors within the rituals in order to illuminate the hidden transcripts. The women leaders in these churches enjoy considerable latitude in the performance of church rituals. The ritual additions, deletions, and maintenance I have described often conform to what Bastide has called the principle of juxtaposition (1978). Other researchers as well as myself have noted the syncretism of African and Christian elements within the two rituals. I am suggesting that such juxtaposition may be understood as an attempt by the women to maximize their power by maintaining the original content of the rituals. The Easter Rock is a case in point. Although women have deleted some of the other songs, they have maintained "Oh David," a traditional chant that pleases the elders and was probably adopted for the ritual because of its biblical and real life meaning to the enslaved Africans. There is also a need, expressed by Ms. Addison and other participants in the community of Winnsboro, "to teach the old ways to the children" (1999). In the case of the Rushin' tradition in the Bahamas, the need was to adopt the new gospelized songs and instruments in order to recruit more young adults into the church and to have a safe and wholesome means of socializing. I have tried to show that ritual adoptions, maintenance, and deletions are solely the prerogatives of the women leaders, whose decisions concerning ritual change are most frequently calculated in the hidden transcripts of preserving the sacred ritual, teaching ritual values, and recruiting young adults.

I suggested in my introduction that there are discrete moments when women find agency within ritual in an otherwise male dominated cultural system. Ritual provides an alternative lens through which to theorize about authority and power within the black folk church. Women in the Easter

Rock as well as the Rushin' tradition are active agents in the cultivation of female authority through developing these various hidden transcripts. Nevertheless, it would be incorrect to conclude that women are denigrated in these two churches. I was repeatedly told that women's contributions are highly valued and that male and female roles are complementary. Just as women cannot run a church on their own, men cannot perform rites of baptism, mourning and other rituals without the help of women. Men and women simply exercise authority under different terms.

NOTES

I would like to express my gratitude to Jill Brody for her insightful comments after reading an early draft of the manuscript. I would also like to thank J. Nash Porter and Mary Lee Eggart for their photographic and graphic skills respectively and the LSU Council on Research for a summer grant to work on this project.

1. Rhyming songs and rhyming spirituals are distinctive types of Bahamian secular work and religious songs. The singing style and performance practices are the same; the words change depending on the context, therefore the repertoire is divided between secular and sacred songs, sacred comprising the majority. "Rhyming" means intoning couplets against a melodic background of voices, although the final syllables of the verses do not necessarily rhyme. "The rhymer—the lead singer—sings a memorized or improvised rhythmic narrative part that continues to build in intensity while the other singers repeat a chorus behind him—that is, they sing the song" (Stecher and Siegel 1990:n.p.). The West African and subsequently the African American tradition of singing or chanting sermons also have influenced this singing style. Clement Bethel (1978) as quoted by D. Gail Saunders in *Slavery in the Bahamas 1648–1838* (Nassau Guardian, 1990) believes that much of the music containing a spiritual quality is derived from the antebellum folk spirituals of the U.S. mainland.

2. A lined-out, long-meter, or Dr. Watts hymn is an older tradition of congregational singing. A deacon or one of the members of the congregation "lined-out," or in the case of black Baptist churches, "raised" the text and melody of the hymn by intoning or chanting a phrase at a time. The congregation followed by singing the words and melody they had just been given. This tradition was very effective in congregations where literacy was rare, however the lining-out style of hymn singing has continued to be a preference among certain congregations. The singing is slow and has a surging choral sound, thus the designation of "long-meter." In addition, in the African American oral tradition, the naming of an entire genre of songs and singing style after a major composer or musician is a way of acknowledging that

a composer or musician set the standard by which all others in that genre will be measured. Dr. Isaac Watts's lyrics resonated within the collective memory of the congregation so that even today the lining-out style is referred to by many as the "Dr. Watts style."

3. In a Baptist church, the phrase "mothers of the church" usually refers to the elderly women who sit in the front pews of the church. They are also referred to as the stewardesses or deaconesses, essentially the female counterpart to the male deacons of the church. These women are charged with the preparation for communion, working with baptismal candidates, praying for the sick and "shut in," and other advisory tasks. They are normally attired in white dresses and hats, if not every Sunday, definitely on communion Sunday. In some churches, these same women belong to "the society," that is, the benevolent society. These societies were established in black communities during Reconstruction and grew out of the need to provide for the sick, properly bury the dead, and care for the families of deceased members. The societies may be female, male, or mixed and many of them still exist today.

4. A vocalist's "signature song" is a song that is frequently performed by one person with a specific stylized version. In the black folk church, when a particular vocalist rises to sing a song, the congregation anticipates a certain culturally sanctioned performance. The song is designated as the singer's and other members of the church usually avoid singing it.

5. Golgotha is the site of the crucifixion, which is referred to as "the place of the skull," in the Bible (St. Matthew 27:33; St. Mark 15:22; and St. John 19:17). The site of the crucifixion is also referred to as Calvary (St. Luke 23:33). The cross was laid on the back of Simon, a Cyrenian, so he could bear it for Jesus (St. Matthew 27:32; St. Mark 15:21; and St. Luke 23:26).

REFERENCES

Bastide. R. 1978 [1960]. *The African Religions of Brazil: Toward a Sociology of the Interpenetration of Civilizations*. Baltimore: Johns Hopkins University Press.

Bell, C. 1997. *Ritual: Perspectives and Dimensions*. New York: Oxford University Press.

Bethel, C. 1978. Music in the Bahamas: Its Roots, Development, and Personality. MA Thesis, University of California, Los Angeles.

———. 1991. *Junkanoo: Festival of the Bahamas*. London: Macmillan.

Blassingame, J. 1979. *The Slave Community: Plantation Life in the Antebellum South*. 2nd ed. New York: Oxford University Press.

Bowie, R. 1995. Personal interview with the author. March 14. Winnsboro, Louisiana.

Boykin, B. 1947. The Folk-Say of Freedom Songs. *New Masses* 65 (October):21.

Brown, S. 1941. Spirituals. In *The Negro Caravan*, ed. S. Brown, A. Gain, and U. Lee. New York: Dryden Press.

———. 1953. Negro Folk Expression: Spirituals, Seculars, Ballads, and Work Songs. *Phylon* 14(1):45–61.

Cash, P., S. Gordon, and G. Saunders. 1991. *Sources of Bahamian History*. London: Macmillan.

Dawson. W. 1955. Interpretation of the Religious Folk-Song of the American Negro. *The Etude* 73 (March).

DuBois, W. E. B. 1961 [1903]. *The Souls of Black Folk*. New York: Fawcett Publication.

Epstein, D. 1977. *Sinful Tunes and Spirituals: Black Folk Music to the Civil War*. Urbana: University of Illinois Press.

Floyd, S. 1991. Ring Shout! Literary Studies, Historical Studies, and Black Music Inquiry. *Black Music Research Journal* 1(11):265–87.

Frey, S., and B. Wood. 1998. *Come Shouting to Zion: African American Protestantism in the American South and British Caribbean to 1830*. Chapel Hill: University of North Carolina Press.

Geggus, D. 1989. The Haitian Revolution. In *The Modern Caribbean*, ed. F. W. Knight and C. A. Palmer. Chapel Hill: University of North Carolina Press.

Gilkes, C. 2001. *"If It Wasn't for the Women . . ." Black Women's Experience and Womanist Culture in Church and Community*. New York: Orbis Books.

Glazier, S. 1983. *Marchin' the Pilgrims Home: Leadership and Decision-Making in an Afro-Caribbean Faith*. West port, Conn.: Greenwood Press.

Gordon, R. 1972. Negro "Shouts" from Georgia. In *Mother Wit from the Laughing Barrel*, ed. A. Dundes. Englewood Cliffs, N.J.: Prentice-Hall.

Gregory, H. 1962. Africa in the Delta. *Louisiana Studies* 1(1):17–23.

Hall, G. 1992. *Africans in Colonial Louisiana: The Development of Afro-Creole Culture in the Eighteenth Century*. Baton Rouge: Louisiana State University Press.

Howard, R. 2002. *Black Seminoles in the Bahamas*. Gainesville: University Press of Florida.

Johnson, H. 1996. *The Bahamas: From Slavery to Servitude, 1783–1933*. Gainesville: University Press of Florida.

Johnson, J., and R. Johnson. 1969 [1925]. Preface. In *The Book of American Negro Spirituals*. New York: Viking Press.

Jones, J. 1996. Personal interview with author. September 14. Monroe, Louisiana.

Jules-Rosette, B. 1989. Privilege Without Power: Women in African Cults and Churches. In *Women in Africa and the African Diaspora*, ed. R. Terborg-Penn and A. Rushing, 99–119. Washington, D.C.: Howard University Press.

Leach, E. 1954. *Political System in Highland Burma: A Study of Kachin Social Structure*. Cambridge, Mass.: Harvard University Press.

———. 1968. Introduction. In *Dialectic in Practical Religion*, ed. E. Leach. Cambridge: Cambridge University Press.

Levine, L. 1977. *Black Culture and Black Consciousness: Afro American Folk Thought From Slavery to Freedom*. New York: Oxford University Press.

Lovell, J. 1972. *Black Song: The Forge and the Flame*. New York: Macmillan.

Mbiti, J. 1969. *African Religions and Philosophy*. New York: Frederick A. Praeger.

Newton, Rev. B. 1996. Personal interview with author. December 28. Red Bays, Andros Island, Bahamas.

Oliver, B., and M. Murphy. 1937. The Works Progress Administration History of Franklin Parish, Louisiana. Unpublished article.

Oster, H. 1957. Play On Your Harp David. *The Harry Collection*. AFS 12575, LWO-5059, Box I, Recorded March 11, 1957, Napoleonville, La. (sung by Rebecca Smith, born in 1885).

———. 1958. Easter Rock Revisited: A Study in Acculturation. *Louisiana Folklore Miscellany* 1(3):21–43.

———, with the Louisiana Folklore Society. n.d. *A Sampler of Louisiana Folksongs, Sung by Traditional Performers*. LSF-1201.

Pitts, W. 1993. *Old Ship of Zion: The Afro-Baptist Ritual in the African Diaspora*. New York: Oxford University Press.

Pollard, M. 1997. Personal interview with author, 29 March, Winnsboro, Louisiana.

Pratt, Pastor M.1996. Personal interview with author. December 28. Conch Sound, Andros Island, Bahamas.

Raboteau, A. 1978. *Slave Religion: The "Invisible Institution" in the Antebellum South*. New York: Oxford University.

Randolph, L. R. 1994. An Ethnobiological Investigation of Andros Island, Bahamas. PhD diss., Miami University.

Rosenbaum, A. 1998. *Shout Because You're Free: The African American Ring Shout Tradition in Coastal Georgia*. Athens: University of Georgia Press.

Saunders, G. 1990 [1985]. *Slavery in the Bahamas 1648–1838*. Nassau: Nassau Guardian.

———. 1993 [1988]. *The Bahamas: A Family of Islands*. 2nd ed. London: MacMillian Press.

———. 1994 [1990]. *Bahamian Society after Emancipation*. Kingston, Jamaica: Ian Randle Publishers.

Saunders, R. 1996. Personal interview with author. December 29. Mastic Point, Andros Island, Bahamas.

Schultz, E., and R. Lavenda. 1998. *Cultural Anthropology: A Perspective on the Human Condition*. New York: West Publishing.

Scott, J. 1990. *Domination and the Arts of Resistance: Hidden Transcripts*. New Haven: Yale University Press.

Seale, L., and M. Seale. 1942. Easter Rock: A Louisiana Negro Ceremony. *Journal of American Folklore* 55:212–18.

Skorupski, J. 1976. *Symbol and Theory: A Philosophical Study of Theories of Religion in Social Anthropology*. New York: Cambridge University Press.

Sobel, M. 1979. *Trabelin On: The Slave Journey to an Afro-Baptist Faith*. Westport, Conn.: Greenwood Press.

Stecher, J., and P. Siegel. 1998 [1966, vol. 1; 1978, vol. 2]. *The Real Bahamas*. Vols. 1 and 2. Nonesuch Records Explorer Series 79300–2.

Stuckey, S. 1987. *Slave Culture: Nationalist Theory and the Foundations of Black America*. New York: Oxford University Press.

Sturman, J. 1993. Asserting Tradition: The Building and Maintenance of African-American Baptist Rock Ceremony in Northeast Louisiana. *Louisiana Folklife* 17:24–45.

Thompson, R. 1984. *Flash of the Spirit: African and Afro-American Art and Philosophy*. New York: Vintage Books.

———. 1981. *The Four Moments of the Sun*. Washington, D.C.: National Gallery of Art.

Where Circum-Caribbean Afro-Catholic Creoles Met American Southern Protestant Conjurers: Origins of New Orleans Voodoo

Martha Ward

New Orleans Voodoo grew from the spiritual and survival complexes that exiled, enslaved Africans brought to Louisiana and fused with the magico-medical knowledge of indigenous Native Americans and the folk theologies and practices of French and Spanish Catholicism. The traditions that evolved through the eighteenth and nineteenth centuries centered on *conjure* —magical transformations of reality—public ceremonials of spirit possession, private rituals of spirit merger, and the social-benevolent societies that Afro-Creole free women of color founded.

Practitioners of New Orleans Voodoo were called "queens," "doctors," or "workers." They addressed both slavery and racism through spirit possession. They knew extensive magical formulas and manipulated the legal system to help slaves escape bondage. The women of Voodoo violated civil codes on "illegal assembly" and put themselves in danger. It is rumored that they succeeded in commuting jail terms for prisoners and abolishing public executions by using spiritual power and political strategies together. They brought a variety of prayers and formulas to social relationships and to undertakings that involved love, luck, or the law.

The use of the word "Voodoo," in various spellings, is part of the scholarly controversy over African "survivals" and spiritual contributions to the New World. The word probably connoted the name of a spirit or deity in one or more West African languages. In New Orleans it became an invocation—a call to spirits. After the 1820s local newspapers used the word to refer to the social group itself, which white people viewed as a cult of "primitive superstitions." Voodoo did not mean "snake worship" to its adherents, although that is a common Anglo interpretation. The word "Voodoo," however, continues to call up racial and sexual stereotypes in contemporary popular usage. Today, the most commonly accepted translation is "those who serve the spirits."

New Orleans Voodoo is related through the diaspora to Candomblé, Macumba, and other Afro-Brazilian religions, to Afro-Caribbean religions like Shango of Trinidad, and to Santería in Cuba. It is not the same thing as Haitian Vodou, Hoodoo in the American South, or Hollywood "voodoo." It is scholarly reductionism or raw diffusionist logic to assume that the spiritual complexes that grew in Louisiana were imported from Africa or the Caribbean like a cargo of rum. Nor were these complexes simple syncretism, a mere reblending of elements like a familiar soup recipe. Louisiana became the link between the very different states of the U.S. South in which it was embedded and the equally evolving slave societies of the Caribbean that it resembled. Therefore, it is necessary—although controversial—to consider the roots of Voodoo in the same light we use to see, as parallel examples, the origins of jazz and the phenomenon of creolization.

French colonial Louisiana was unique in the annals of the African diaspora. The majority of the African founders of the colony of Louisiana came directly from West and Central Africa. Contrary to common assumptions, they did not pass through the Caribbean first. Africans in colonial Louisiana outnumbered the less powerful Europeans two to one and brought skills in metallurgy, tropical agriculture, indigo production, irrigation, marketing, and medical care. Their imported cultural knowledge was crucial to the survival of the struggling colony. The largest group consisted of Bambara speakers from Senegambia (Hall 1992; Hanger 1997). The next largest contingent came directly to Louisiana from the Kingdom of Kongo. Many were already Christians, well versed in Catholic catechism and religious traditions (Hall 1992:275–315; Thornton 1987–1988). Africans carried embodied knowledge of public dances of spirit possession, songs, bands, musical instruments like drum, banjos, and tambourines directly to French Louisiana. They developed extensive practices of "master magic" called *gris-gris*, a potion or spell to help or harm someone. *Gris-gris* is the Voodoo name for conjure; its folk cognate is *ju-ju*. Court cases in 1743 and 1773 acknowledged both the existence and effectiveness of *gris-gris* or conjure in eighteenth-century colonial Louisiana (Porteus 1934). These cases and many that followed led to accusations that practitioners were poisoners and sorcerers. Diverse documents, however, reveal that concepts of magical empowerment with the direct help of spiritual forces were deeply rooted in the Afro-Creole worldview.

Slavery in Louisiana did not look like slavery in the rest of the U.S. South or in the Caribbean. Slaves were not always black, and blacks were not always slaves. French and Spanish colonial administrations feared uprisings and African-Indian alliances. They developed liberal policies of emancipation and manumission and permitted regular and largely unrestrained public dances or ritual celebrations in places like Congo Square in New Orleans. Frenchmen took African and Native American women as slaves, companions, mistresses, employees, and wives. Free women of color in New Orleans outnumbered both white women and slave women; they became leaders in the Catholic Church and in the community. The women knew home health care—herbs, teas, poultices, bandaging, diagnosis, and treatment. They produced food, marketed it, and provisioned their families. In each generation women of color schemed to buy themselves, their children, and other family members out of slavery. Their activism led to the largest community of *gens de couleur libre* or free people of color in the United States and to the spiritual complexes labeled Voodoo. In south Louisiana the intersection of sex and race forged a New World people called Creoles. Voodoo, jazz, dances, cuisine, and architecture have Creole roots. In New Orleans during the colonial and early national periods, "Creole" referred to the culture and cuisine of native-born, largely endogamous, French-speaking Catholics of all colors.

When Reconstruction ended in 1877, Jim Crow—the doctrine of separate-but-equal and the cornerstone of American apartheid—began. "Creole" became a contested racial category. Today the term "Creole" is at the center of intense public controversies over the politics of color and who can or cannot claim its heritage (Kein 2000; Hirsch and Logsdon 1992; Dominguez 1994).

There are four major sources of information about New Orleans Voodoo: 1. The staff of the WPA Federal Writers' Project in Louisiana, part of the Depression recovery programs of the 1930s, interviewed several hundred citizens including people who had been previously enslaved (Clayton 1990) and many who had known the practitioners of Voodoo. The interviews are housed in various state archives. 2. Zora Neale Hurston, novelist, anthropologist, and folklorist, did field research in New Orleans from 1929 to 1930. An African American and graduate student in anthropology at Columbia University, Hurston was initiated into New Orleans Voodoo at least six times, the last time with a man whom she believed to be the grandnephew of Marie Laveau the Second. Her lyrical descriptions of these ceremonies are the best in the Voodoo-Hoodoo literature (1931; 1990:198–205). 3. Harry Middleton Hyatt, an eccentric Episcopalian priest turned folklorist, privately published five volumes of interviews with southern practitioners of what he called "hoodoo, witchcraft, root-work, and conjuration." Between 1938 and 1940 Hyatt interviewed about thirty to forty practitioners and clients in New Orleans (1970, 1973, 1978). 4. White journalists, travelers, and regional writers in the nineteenth century published accounts in newspapers, books, and magazines.

The major spiritual imperatives of New Orleans Voodoo center on protection and freedom. Practitioners focused their spiritual intentions and magical strategies on social relationships—owners and slaves; bosses and workers; husbands and wives; lovers; neighbors; in-laws; and policemen, judges, and lawyers. Voodoo theology acknowledged and provided rituals to contact ancestors, Catholic saints, or other "natural" people who were once human. Other spirits were invoked in times of desperate need or suffering; some spirits volunteered their help through visions, mergers, or possessions.

The best known priestesses or practitioners of New Orleans Voodoo were Marie Laveau the First and Marie Laveau the Second, mother and daughter. Marie Laveau the First, also known as "the Widow Paris," was born in 1801; she died on June 16, 1881, and is buried in St. Louis Cemetery Number One, New Orleans' most historic "city of the dead." She had a high social standing as a Creole fever nurse and was an active member of St. Louis Cathedral and a counselor to men on death row in Parish prison. In these capacities, she did shamanic and liturgical forms of psychopomp work for the dying, and she did conjure work to free prisoners or allow them a merciful death at a time when hangings were a spectator sport. Her known spiritual signatures were fire, the great serpent or *Le Grand Zombi*, St. Anthony, and the Virgin Mary.

Marie Laveau the Second, also known as Eucharist Glapion, was born February 2, 1827; she had disappeared by 1877—no reliable date of death, cause of death, or burial site for her are known. People speculated and gossiped about her; well into the twenty-first century, some in the community swore that she drowned and rose again. She was probably a hairdresser and ran a spiritual practice out of her home, calling in spirits to counsel citizens about matters such as unfaithful husbands, disloyal friends, gambling reverses, bad bosses, ungrateful children, and court cases. On each June 23, St. John's Eve, Marie the Second planned and led interracial Voodoo ceremonials and parties at locations along the beaches of Lake Pontchartrain. Her known spiritual signatures were water, St. John the Baptist, High John the Conqueror, and the Good Mother.

Both women were French-speaking Catholics, leaders in the Afro-Creole community, and both bore the children of men they could not marry. The mother and daughter have been routinely confused with each other throughout the nineteenth and twentieth centuries. Both Laveaus and many other free women of color for whom records exist maintained elaborate altars in their homes. They placed candles, holy or blessed water, offerings of food, legal documents or letters, statues to Catholic saints, spices or chemical compounds, and other ritual materials on them. When a client came with a problem, the priestess went to her altar and prayed, journeyed, or otherwise entered into an altered state of consciousness. Once in that state she merged with a spirit who then spoke through her to the troubled client. The best published accounts of these spiritual sessions come from the thirty long prayers or "Psalms of Voodoo" that Zora Neale Hurston collected (Hurston 1931). As the grandnephew of Marie the Second explained to her, "Marie Laveau is not a woman when she answer the one who ask. No. She is a god, yes. Whatever she say, it will come so" (Hurston 1990:195).

Conjure—the magical means to transform reality—was an important shamanic activity of New Orleans Voodoo. In the African American worldview, conjure means using language and ritual to link magical and supernatural elements with medicinal practices and natural processes. Conjure produces two realities or states of consciousness and mediates between them. Conjurers have both worldly and spiritual insight. Voodoo or Hoodoo practitioners in the U.S. South often called themselves "two-headed doctors" —one head for consensual realities and the other for spiritual realms. In Eurocentric reasoning, however, conjure became synonymous with overheated imaginations at best and with witchcraft or sorcery at worst.

Voodoo practitioners earned a formidable reputation for their abilities to contact the spirits of deceased people. Women's social lives revolved around funerals, mourning rituals, and the annual observances of death. Infant mortality in New Orleans was exceptionally high, medical care almost nonexistent. Extensive Catholic and Creole mourning customs prescribed regular visits to family graves and encouraged prayerful contact with dead relatives and friends. A powerful and easily obtained ingredient in Voodoo magical formulas is graveyard dust. The etiquette of visiting and cleaning graves in the cemeteries shaded easily into psychopomp work where the souls of the dead were consulted, consoled, and conducted to better places. These spiritual traditions are still practiced in New Orleans, where the cemeteries are major tourist attractions.

Since New Orleans Voodoo lives in the shadow of its larger and more famous relative, Haitian Vodou, it has been assumed that the spirits each honored were the same. The pantheon in Haiti, however, contained thousands of interrelated spirits, addressed far more aspects of social and spiritual life, and had more direct connections to West Africa than did the roll call of spirits in New Orleans. The *Lwa* (also spelled Loa) or spirits of Haiti begin with Danbala (in various spellings), the great serpent, and Ayida-Wedo, rainbow mistress of the sky, who form the world's first couple. Greatly beloved Papa Legba is the cosmic gatekeeper; Ezulie (also spelled Erzulie or Ezili) has two female forms—Freda, the spirit of lovers everywhere, and Dant, a dark-skinned, jealous single mother. Ogou, the warrior, is actually a family of spirits who embodies the realm of male-centered activities: war, politics, machinery, metalworking, and fire. In New Orleans, Haiti, Cuba, and all the circum-Caribbean sites where similar spiritual practices grew, all these spirits of place and purpose answer to God, *Le Bon Dieu* (in various spellings and pronunciations). Throughout the islands and coasts of the Caribbean, the spirits of the diaspora also have strong and equivalent Catholic identities. In Haiti for example, Legba is St. Peter and St. Anthony; Ezulie is Mater Dolorosa and the Black Madonna in Haiti, and corresponds to Our Lady of Prompt Succor in New Orleans.

In New Orleans, however, a place-specific pantheon arose dominated by a female spirit in direct contact with the Good God, or *Bon Dié* in Louisiana Creole French. This woman is variously called the Holy Mother, the Virgin Mary, the Good Mother, Madonna, Mother-of-All, "lovely Lady dressed in blue," or Lady Luck. In the person of Our Lady of Prompt Succor she saved the city from British armies at the Battle of New Orleans in 1815 and from menacing fires and hurricanes on many other occasions. Other saints, particularly St. Anthony and St. John the Baptist, are still honored in local traditions, both Catholic and Voodoo. Folk records also mention St. Peter, St. Rita, St. Michael, and St. Joseph. The most popular saint of New Orleans—one not limited to Voodoo—is St. Expedite who makes things happen quickly. Swift action is a special blessing, even a miracle. The spirits and saints of New Orleans Voodoo are earthy spiritual helpers; they respond to written instructions, forceful prayers, intense suffering, and personal sacrifice. Mirroring well-known qualities of Louisiana politics, they are also known to take bribes and make deals (Hurston 1931; Hyatt 1978, 1973, 1970).

The Laveaus and other priestesses danced with snakes and called on a serpent spirit named *Le Grand Zombi* in their spirit possession rituals. The origin of the name is unclear. For African Christians from the Kingdom of Kongo, the name of God was *Zambi a Mpungu*; in St. Domingue-Haiti, a zombi is a person raised from the dead, a person whose immortal soul has been stolen. In New Orleans, however, the Great Zombi seems to have been a fierce spirit of resistance and protest embodied in possession. Although these spirits and saints have obvious parallels in Africa or in Haiti, names like Danbala-Damballah (in various spellings) for the serpent spirit or Erzulie-Ezili for the female spirit are not found in existing documentary sources for Louisiana.

Everything in New Orleans Voodoo bowed before intention and desire. A person's name was the chief ingredient of their identity, the essence of their living spirits. Wishes, prayers, blessings, or curses were spoken aloud or written down with a person's name and the intention attached. Holy water and candles, among other spiritual artifacts, set the intention. Nothing in New Orleans Voodoo happened "naturally" or because it was "meant to be." There was no such thing as fate, coincidence, serendipity, or acausal synchronicity. Good luck and bad luck were not whims of the spirit world. They resulted from manipulation, maneuvering, magic, and the intentions and ritual actions of a master magician. Each practitioner used his or her own spiritual experiences to contact the spirits for advice. A practitioner could accomplish the same goal in any of a half dozen ways. New or different remedies to solve the same problem were not lies—not "made up on the spot." In Voodoo theology, there were no "either-or" commandments, good or bad moral choices. Pictures of saints doused with holy water, for example, could hurt people or help them, depending on the intention the user set.

Voodoo practitioners earned a reputation for "fixing" or putting a curse on those who crossed them. They knew how to make their enemies ill or even kill them if necessary. The voodoo dolls sold in the French Quarter pay testimony to these abilities, although there is no historical evidence that practitioners like the Laveaus ever made or employed such dolls. These objects are probably more mercantile imagination than spiritual fact. Nonetheless, even ordinary citizens in New Orleans knew and gossiped about various recipes or prescriptions that used common household materials and prayers to wound others. In the logic of Voodoo, however, the curse will rebound on the curser. If one can send misfortune to an enemy, a competitor, a rival, a bad boss, or an ex-lover, then they can in turn send it back. Spiritual power sent without compassion returns to injure the sender.

Without regular sanctuaries or congregation houses, the Voodoo orders met in parks, private homes, in businesses closed for the night, and at the bayous, swamps, or lakes near the city. The most important site was Congo Square, an open plaza on the northern boundary of the French Quarter (Johnson 1995; Cable 1976). Historic evidence shows that African-born enslaved and free people danced there on Sunday afternoons from the mid 1700s to the late 1850s when authorities succeeded in closing it. Congo Square was a major market center, dance arena, community gathering spot, and ritual space—the crossroads, the pivot of Afro-Creole life, the epicenter of its mystical geography. Scholars regard it as the cradle of African American esthetics, modern dance in America, jazz, and New Orleans Voodoo (Kmen 1972; Anderson 1960; and Federal Writers' Project). White people witnessed black people gathered in large numbers to do something that to them resembled religion. Journalists, travelers, and regional writers left eyewitness accounts of bands and their instruments, choruses, songs, ring dances, and spirit possession. The featured performers were women of color in loose white dresses and *tignons*, the headdresses or turbans Creole women of color wore in defiance of an edict that forbade them to wear bonnets like white Creole women.

No place in America is more directly associated with the roots of jazz than is Congo Square. Some scholars say that the ritual dances of the Voodoos, called the "Congo dance" or the "Creole dance," were the crucible of modern American dance (Johnson 1995; Emery 1988). Women remained within their own tight circles and undulated in sinuous motions resembling snakes. Sometimes the Voodoo practitioners danced with snakes, probably the nonpoisonous Louisiana *Coluber* species. With feet flat, a dancer slowly shifted her weight from one ankle to her thighs and then to her hips and torso as she imitated the movements of snakes who have no legs. The women did not move their feet from the ground as they swayed in undulatory motions from ankles to shoulders. Men mimicked fighting as they danced in circles around the women who performed the constricted ankle-thigh-hip-shoulder step of the classic Voodoo ritual dance. They leaped into the air and performed feats of gymnastic dancing. They had bands of bells attached to each leg and at some dances balanced bottles or carafes filled with alcoholic spirits on their heads. A chorus of those who knew the songs accompanied the dancers and the musicians. The orchestra or band set the beat with their often-handmade instruments. Typically, the players had at least one large drum made from a wooden barrel covered with a cured animal skin and played with animal bones as beaters. There are reliable historic accounts of banjos and other stringed instruments, tambourines, and rattles made from gourds.

This description includes the ritual dances, music, calendrical ceremonies, and initiation services of the Voodoo orders as well as what were probably secular Afro-Creole celebrations as well. The sexual excitement and spiritual power on these occasions are evident even in scandalized or confused eyewitness accounts. Witnesses reported chant-style songs, call-and-response lyrics, and a liturgical pacing of rituals from invocation to ritual release. Congo Square must be interpreted as a site of resistance and confrontation as well as creativity and spiritual evolution.

The two most significant holy days of New Orleans Voodoo are November 1, the Day of the Dead or All Saints Day, and June 23, St. John's Eve. Both are associated with Catholic as well as pre-Christian celebrations and probably African ones as well. The Day of the Dead follows All Hallows Eve, or Halloween, and in New Orleans is called All Saints Day. It has become part of the elaborate masking and celebratory traditions of civil society. To honor their dead and have a party, citizens of the city visit family tombs, make offerings, clean up, communicate with the dead, and honor their ancestors. The night of June 23 at midsummer honors St. John the Baptist and High John the Conqueror, a major folk hero-spirit of southern Hoodoo whose influence in New Orleans is well documented (Hurston 1931, 1990). The Voodoo gatherings were typically opened by a priestess who rapped on the floor or ground three times—people said that this meant "Father, Son, and Holy Spirit" or "Faith, Hope, and Charity." Since 1998 Voodoo houses in New Orleans have joined with others throughout the southern United States and the circum-Caribbean to add "hurricane-turning" ceremonies to their ceremonial calendar; in New Orleans these annual shamanic dances to influence the course of tropical weather systems are held in July.

Nineteenth-century New Orleans had the highest mortality rates, the deadliest epidemics, and the worst public health system in the United States. The city's subtropical climate and below-sea-level location, chronic lack of leadership, and appalling sanitation led to yellow fever, cholera, malaria, fulminating dysenteries, and other diseases (Duffy 1962). The population depended on "fever nurses"—women of color who had learned skills from female relatives and who used extremely varied techniques from African, Haitian, and American Indian ancestors. "Nursing women" like

Marie Laveau the First were routinely identified as Voodoo practitioners; their skills were widely regarded as contributions to community survival.

Women of color in New Orleans practiced an effective array of alternative, integrated, or holistic medicine. Besides their documented bedside skills, they had an extensive pharmacopoeia. Historic records mention ginseng, gum balsam, jalap, rhubarb, snakeroot, sarsaparilla, St. John's wort, sassafras, copal tree, maidenhair ferns, cottonwood roots, acacia leaves, elderberry bark, sage, Indian hemp, holly leaves, and hundreds more plants and plant parts, many purchased at Native American markets. The first licensed pharmacist in America opened a French-style pharmacy in 1823 and ordered many materials and compounds from New York or Paris.

The practitioners of New Orleans Voodoo had an extensive pharmacopoeia of chemicals and compounds which they mixed and used primarily for conjure or magical work rather than for individual healing. In the Voodoo section of the French pharmacy, there were oils of cinnamon, cassia, bergamot, "Sanguinaria Aragon" or dragon's blood, antimony, iron wire, coffee beans, verbena, lemon grass, cochineal, guinea peppers, lodestones, cayenne pepper, iron filings, kerosene, elm bark tea, St. John's root, and many other classic ingredients as well. The pharmacist sold love, luck, and control over capricious fate under various names: Love Success, Lucky Devil, As You Please, Attraction, and the famous Love Potion Number Nine. The shelves held some of Voodoo's trademark formulas for a successful social life: Get-away Powder, Waste-away Tea, War Waters, the Essence of Three Thieves, and the Goddess of Evils. There were a wide assortment of powders whose name reveals its intention—dragging powders, stay-away powder, separation powder, confusement powder, disturbment powder, whirlwind powders, moving-on powders, and hot-foot powder. These Voodoo materials were as conventional for that period as those the white medical establishment favored—harsh laxatives and purgatives, mercury, arsenic, or black leeches to suck blood (Long 2001; Hurston 1990; Hyatt 1970, 1973, 1978; Federal Writers' Project). But the local treatments were probably more effective, reflecting a creative, woman-based syncretism throughout the U.S. South and circum-Caribbean.

Other than these formulas and compounds, still widely available in the spiritual botanicas and corner grocery stores of the city, no known artifacts of New Orleans Voodoo have survived. The police confiscated cartloads of ritual objects in raids during the 1850s and did not return them.

Several waves of migration gradually reshaped and shaded into New Orleans Voodoo in the nineteenth century. In 1809 a group of about ten thousand French-speaking Catholic Creoles came to New Orleans from St. Domingue, renamed Haiti after a successful revolution brought former slaves to positions of power on the island. These "foreign French" mirrored the demographic structure by age, gender, and condition of servitude, roughly doubling the population of the city. The new Creoles did not bring the complex which scholars now know as Haitian Vodou to New Orleans; they did add artisanal and architectural skills, a better assortment of bridegrooms and bakeries, and a fierce identity as Creoles—French-speaking Catholics with a lust for wine, dancing, fine cuisine, horse-racing, and a marriage system that bordered on bigamy. They enhanced similar Afro-Creole traditions already present and contributed greatly to the French qualities of the city in the period when Anglos and Protestants were passing laws to Americanize it (Lachance 1992). At the same time, the émigrés adjusted to their adopted city and over time blended with the local population. Folklore sources claim that Sanité Dede from St. Domingue initiated the young Marie the First into Voodoo; it is also clear from the surviving prayers, songs, and ritual dances that the New Orleans Creole world, not Haiti, was Marie's crucible of spirituality.

The social and religious contexts of Vodou in St. Domingue–Haiti and Voodoo in New Orleans were not the same. A black revolution built and exploded in St. Domingue, leaving an independent black nation. In Louisiana, American racial laws and tensions over slavery intensified in slow steps, leading ultimately to a civil war between white people of different regions (Hunt 1988). In the new nation of Haiti, cut off from trade and commerce with the remainder of America and Europe for decades, Vodou was the primary unifying structure; it expanded to fill the gaps and survival imperatives of civil society. In New Orleans in the meantime and in a milder atmosphere, Voodoo groups became community-benevolent organizations and sites for covert resistance to intensifying codes and laws of racial apartheid.

The second wave of influence in New Orleans Voodoo came from southern blacks who had—largely in secret—developed elaborate systems of conjure, "master magic," and hands-on healing from their experiences with the plantocracy and slavery systems of the rural South. These powerful traditions are generally called Hoodoo in the literature and rarely appreciated in popular or scholarly consciousness (Hurston 1990; Hyatt 1978, 1973, 1970). In the two decades before the Civil War and increasingly after Emancipation in 1863, English-speaking and evangelical or ecstatic Protestants, like the earlier French-speaking Catholic Haitians, changed and were changed by New Orleans. Historians and anthropologists have difficulty teasing out the contributions of southern African Americans after the Civil War and the folk Catholicism of Italian and Irish immigrants after the 1840s to the French Afro-Creole foundations of New Orleans (Dominguez 1994; Hirsch and Logsdon 1992; Kein 2000).

In 1877, Reconstruction and the federal occupation of New Orleans ended. The era of American apartheid called Jim Crow, "separate but equal" segregation, began. Local press and police escalated their attacks on the women of Voodoo. Legislators at both state and local levels passed and enforced strict laws against "fortune-telling," spiritual counseling, or any psychic activities that promoted good luck. Newspapers continued to recycle stories about orgies, boiling caldrons, "black" magic, and human or animal sacrifice. Hundreds of post-Laveau practitioners moved or were exiled to Algiers, a suburb across the Mississippi river from New Orleans proper.

At the beginning of the twentieth century, African American women started a unique group of churches in New Orleans, the Spiritual Churches —not to be confused with Spiritualism or the Spiritualist Movement. These churches were syncretic, based on native African spirit contacts through possession, an Afro-centric identification with Zionism, Israel, and the Israelites, native North American Indian traditions, fundamentalist and ecstatic Christianity, nineteenth-century Spiritualism, and charismatic Catholicism (Jacobs and Kaslow 1991). Practitioners today use titles such as spiritual advisors, palm readers, fortune-tellers, psychics, spiritual readers, prophets, or Reverend Mothers. Sometimes they speak of themselves or others speak of them as healers or healing mediums. They avoid words like conjurer, doctor, queen, or root-worker. Groups of women continue in the tradition of altars, personal adoration, contacts with saints and spirits, and sacramental services of initiation and baptism. They honor ancestors like "Mother Laveau." They build elaborate altars with candles, pictures of saints and spirit guides, photographs or statues of respected Indian chiefs, crucifixes, holy water, food, flowers, perfume, incense, rosaries, and letters to spirits. Spiritual Churches provide an alternative to racism and internalized oppression; they offer direct experiences with the spirit world. The leaders of the Spiritual Churches point with pride to their Afro-Catholic roots. But they cannot afford to acknowledge their kinship with New Orleans Voodoo.

Sometime in the late nineteenth century, in Spiritual Churches and the remnants of the post-Laveau Voodoo orders operating under civil sanctions, a Native American revolutionary figure, Black Hawk, joined the pantheon of place-specific spirits in New Orleans. Since then, African American men in New Orleans have dressed or "masked" as Native American warriors in tribute to Black Hawk and traditions of resistance. Calling themselves Mardi Gras Indians, they lead street marches and dances in elaborate feathered and sequined costumes. By the middle of the twentieth century, they had taken the place of the women of Voodoo in their spirited public ceremonialism and resistance to racial oppression.

Although the trajectory of Voodoo through the last half of the twentieth century is difficult to reconstruct, my interviews reveal that post-Laveau practitioners were still initiating men and women into the practices of indigenous New Orleans Voodoo well into the 1950s. It is clear, however, that whatever crucible of change the spiritual traditions underwent during exile and segregation, they began to revive by the 1990s. Prior to this revival women and men had to travel to Haiti or West Africa to learn the liturgies and songs and receive the shamanic training they needed. Since then, several houses or congregations have formed, and practitioners are actively initiating new members locally. Several sturdy peristyles have been built and dedicated, and local spirits and observances added to those imported from Haiti, a contemporary reconnection to the island. A half-dozen houses stage dances on Bayou St. John, in parks, private homes, and Congo Square for their members, and invite tourists, anthropologists, filmmakers, and an increasingly appreciative and largely white audience. Local practitioners have published books that link New Orleans to Haiti, Cuba, Africa, the U.S. South, and New Age or counterculture movements in increasingly creative and accessible ways (Glassman 2000; Teish 1985; Calder 2002; Martinié and Glassman 1992).

Observers of nineteenth-century New Orleans Voodoo were always struck by the number of white women participating in ritual dances and seeking counseling from the priestesses. In the contemporary revivals white and white middle-class adherents—again, mostly female—are more in evidence than African American visitors expect. Voodoo in New Orleans was more multicolored, always crossed class and ethnic lines more fluidly, than its counterparts in the Caribbean and the U.S. South—it was stigmatized because it embodied a transcendent dream of racial justice. In the twenty-first-century, Voodoo has as many theological and personal connections to New Age and feminist spiritualities in the United States as to diasporan identities or ethnicity. Voodoo as it is currently evolving in New Orleans is not the static lineal descendant of earlier forms from the Caribbean and southern United States; it is the organic outgrowth and transformation within the kinship of the diaspora, the worldwide outreach of the Catholic church, and, above all, the unique survival imperatives and spiritual connections forged at the foot of the Mississippi River.

REFERENCES

Anderson, J. 1960. The New Orleans Voodoo Ritual Dance and Its Twentieth Century Survivals. *Southern Folklore Quarterly* 24:135–43.

Cable, G. 1976. *The Dance in Place Congo and Creole Slave Songs*. 3rd ed. New Orleans, La.: Faruk von Turk.

Calder, S. 2002. Mark of Voodoo: Awakening to My African Spiritual Heritage. St. Paul, Minn.: Llewellyn Publications.

Clayton, R. 1990. *Mother Wit: The Ex-slave Narratives of the Louisiana Writers' Project*. New York: Peter Lang.

Domínguez, V. 1994. *White By Definition: Social Classification in Creole Louisiana*. New Brunswick, N.J.: Rutgers University Press.

Duffy, J. 1958, 1962. *The Rudolph Matas History of Medicine in Louisiana*. Vols. 1 and 2. Baton Rouge: Louisiana State University.

Emery, L. 1988. *Black Dance From 1619 To Today*. 2nd ed. Princeton, N.J.: Dance Horizons Press.

Federal Writers' Project. Archives of the Works Progress Administration, Federal Writers' Project of Louisiana, Cammie G. Henry Research Center, Northwestern State University, Natchitoches, Louisiana; and State Library of Louisiana, Baton Rouge, Louisiana (unpublished, no dates).

Glassman, S. 2000. *Vodou Visions: An Encounter with Divine Mystery*. New York: Villard.

Hall, G. 1992. *Africans in Colonial Louisiana: The Development of Afro-Creole Culture in the Eighteenth Century*. Baton Rouge: Louisiana State University Press.

Hanger, K. 1997. *Bounded Lives, Bounded Places: Free Black Society in Colonial New Orleans, 1769–1803*. Durham: Duke University Press.

Hirsch, A., and J. Logsdon, eds. 1992. *Creole New Orleans: Race and Americanization*. Baton Rouge: Louisiana State University Press.

Hunt, A. 1988. *Haiti's Influence on Antebellum America: Slumbering Volcano in the Caribbean*. Baton Rouge: Louisiana State University Press.

Hurston, Z. 1931. Hoodoo in America. *Journal of American Folklore* 44(174): 317–417.

———. 1990. *Mules and Men*. New York: HarperPerennial.

Hyatt, H. 1978, 1973, 1970. *Hoodoo—Conjuration—Witchcraft—Rootwork*. Vols. 1–5. Hannibal, Mo.: Western Publishing.

Jacobs, C., and A. Kaslow. 1991. *The Spiritual Churches of New Orleans: Origins, Beliefs, and Rituals of an African-American Religion*. Knoxville: University of Tennessee Press.

Johnson, J. 1995. *Congo Square in New Orleans*. New Orleans: Louisiana Landmarks Society.

Kein, S., ed. 2000. *Creole: The History and Legacy of Louisiana's Free People of Color*. Baton Rouge: Louisiana State University Press.

Kmen, H. 1972. The Roots of Jazz and the Dance in Place Congo: A Re-appraisal. *Yearbook, Anuario 8*, Institute of Latin American Studies, University of Texas, Austin.

Lachance, P. 1992. The Foreign French. In *Creole New Orleans: Race and Americanization*, ed. Hirsch and Logsdon, 101–130. Baton Rouge: Louisiana State University Press.

Long, C. 2001. *Spiritual Merchants: Religion, Magic, and Commerce*. Knoxville: University of Tennessee Press.

Martinié, L., and S. Glassman. 1992. *The New Orleans Voodoo Tarot*. Rochester, Vt.: Destiny Books.

Porteous, L. 1934. The Gris-Gris Case. *Louisiana Historical Quarterly* 17(1):48–63.

Teish, L. 1885. *Jambalaya: The Natural Woman's Book of Personal Charms and Practical Rituals*. New York: HarperSanFrancisco.

Thornton, J. 1987–88. On the Trail of Voodoo: African Christianity in Africa and the Americas. *Americas* 44(3):261–78.

Race, Class, and Environmental Justice: Eastern Caribbean Dimensions of a "Southern" Problem

Mark Moberg

A NEW SPECIES OF TROUBLE

The African experience in the Caribbean and the southern United States has been forged from many common traumas during and since the three centuries of the Middle Passage. Chattel slavery, plantation labor, sharecropping, forced migration, and a pervasive and persistent color bar have been features common throughout the African diaspora, whether in Alabama or Antigua. Such commonalities continued long past the demise of the plantation-based economies in which black labor provided the motive force. In the mid-twentieth century, the common restrictions placed on political life and economic opportunity for Africans in the Americas found simultaneous expression in the movements for independence that swept the Caribbean and the movement for civil rights in the United States. Black nationalism, a component of the civil rights movement and an ideology introduced into the United States by Marcus Garvey, came full circle a generation later as migrants returning from the United States brought the ideas of Martin Luther King Jr. and Malcolm X back to the islands. Clearly, then, the many historical convergences in regional experience favor myriad social, political, and even geographic comparisons between the Caribbean and the U.S. South.

Within this comparative framework, what is to be made of the environmental justice movement, the most recent collective expression of African American aspirations for equality? As a social movement, environmental justice traces its origins to a 1984 public protest against the dumping of hazardous waste in a black community of North Carolina, a protest that spontaneously fused the strategy of nonviolent civil disobedience with environmental concerns about a polluting landfill. Since then, in a creative synthesis drawing upon sociological research, grassroots protest, and alliances with progressive lawyers, the movement has revitalized environmental and civil rights constituencies whose causes were viewed as increasingly moribund and bureaucratic by the 1980s (Dowie 1995). In addition to its growth as a social movement, environmental justice has generated an extensive array of academic studies linking pollution exposure to race and class (United Church of Christ 1987; Bullard 1990). In 1994 the Clinton administration embraced the issue as an article of national policy by requiring all federal agencies and federally funded programs to address their environmental impact on low-income and minority populations (see Bullard 1996:498). The grassroots protests and legal challenges mounted under the new federal policies have compelled polluting industries to at least rhetorically address the issue of equity in environmental quality. In some highly publicized instances, such challenges have forced the cancellation or relocation of industrial projects that threatened the environmental well-being of low-income communities (Allen 2003). The movement has also forced a once almost entirely white and largely upper-middle-class environmental movement to acknowledge the concerns of minority and working-class communities (Di Chiro 1992).

If environmental racism is but one manifestation of the disadvantaged political and economic status of African Americans, can the same be said of African people in the Caribbean? What is the utility of the environmental justice paradigm for understanding environmental problems in the Caribbean, and can it provide a template for social movements throughout the region? In the United States, the environmental justice movement is a product of what sociologist Kai Erikson (1994) calls "a new species of trouble," the unanticipated and largely unknowable dangers lurking in our air, water, and soil as a byproduct of the industrial growth once heralded as the very measure of high modernity. In its synthesis of identity politics and disillusion with the ostensible benefits of smokestack industry, environmental justice has emerged as a postmodern social movement par excellence. Its proponents have targeted for closure or relocation toxic waste sites, polluting factories, and incinerators, all associated with some aspect of heavy modern industrial development. For such activists, the material benefits traditionally associated with heavy industry (primarily employment) were no longer deemed to be worth the steep long-term costs in public health paid by low-income communities. In part, this recognition stems from the fact that a good deal of industrial manufacturing, which once generated much of the employment for relatively unskilled minority workers, had moved abroad by the 1980s. Instead, polluted minority communities such as those of the "cancer corridor" along the Mississippi River north of New Orleans found themselves hosts to capital-intensive chemical plants and PVC manufacturers that recruited skilled workers from elsewhere (Moberg 2001: 173).

ENVIRONMENTAL INJUSTICE IN THE CARIBBEAN: A BRIEF HISTORY

At first consideration, it may appear that the environmental justice paradigm is of limited or no utility to the Caribbean islands. Unlike the industrialization that spawned the environmental justice movement, agriculture has traditionally been the Caribbean's economic lifeblood, now supplemented by remittances from migrants residing in North America and Europe, tourism, and a brisk underground trade in illicit drugs. Nor is it easy to find direct counterparts of the degraded landscapes of North America's manufacturing centers in the island Caribbean. The Caribbean that presents itself to the public imagination is that of the tourist literature: an idyllic setting of pristine waters and beaches, vibrant coral reefs, and dense inland rainforests, all of which betray little or no environmental despoliation.

In actuality, the incorporation of the region into the world system since the sixteenth century has had a devastating environmental cost. Further, these costs have been distributed in a highly inequitable fashion among the populations that have occupied the Caribbean, although such injustices have rarely been described as environmental in nature. The ecological consequences of European conquest were immediate and irreversible and were expressed most dramatically through the extirpation of virtually all indigenous populations in the Caribbean. Horrified colonial-era chroniclers such as Fray Bartolome de Las Casas systematically documented the mistreatment of Caribbean Amerindians forced to mine gold for the Spanish (Las Casas 1992) and attributed the decimation of native populations to such practices. It is likely, however, that Old World pathogens such as smallpox, measles, and malaria, to which indigenous populations lacked any acquired immunity, exacted a much greater toll than did European abuses. By 1524, all of the native populations of the Greater Antilles and the Bahamas, as well as most of those of the Lesser Antilles, had been exterminated in the course of virgin-field epidemics (Watts 1995).

As native populations died out, their agricultural lands were abandoned and quickly reverted to forest cover, a process that occurred in other former aboriginal areas of the Americas as well (Lentz 2000). In the Caribbean, most traces of native agriculture and even settlements were consumed by secondary forest within decades of native depopulation. Barbados, for example, had been one of the most heavily populated of the Lesser Antilles during the Precolumbian period. Yet one hundred years after the demise of the native population, the island's first English settlers encountered nothing but dense forests growing down to the shoreline. While the Spanish introduced many nonnative plant species into the region, most were initially unable to establish themselves in the new environment, primarily because of direct competition with the encroaching forest or because of the lack of available space within it. Nonnative plants did not gain a foothold until later when forests were removed to make way for sugarcane. Introduced animal species, however, multiplied rapidly in habitats that lacked natural predators and competing species. The Spanish left pigs on nearly every island as a potential food source for colonists, and these animals adapted readily to Caribbean forests. By 1514, over thirty thousand hogs, most of them wild, were reported on Cuba. Pigs, in particular, competed with the declining native human population and may have hastened its demise by rooting up *canucos* and destroying native crops. Spanish cattle also thrived on Caribbean islands, further compounding long-term environmental problems. The hooves of both cattle and pigs compacted the soil along their trackways, resulting in severe gully erosion in the form of *barrancas* on Cuba and Hispañola by the late sixteenth century (Moberg 2004).

As readily accessible sources of gold were depleted together with the native peoples compelled to mine it, Crown authorities sought other sources of wealth by the late sixteenth century. Throughout the Caribbean, European settlers turned to an array of agricultural commodities. Tobacco, cotton, indigo, and ginger were introduced with varying levels of success, typically among the few thousand European yeoman farmers who settled in the region. None of these crops so thoroughly transformed human-environmental relations in the Caribbean as did sugarcane (Mintz 1985). First domesticated in Asia from a wild grass species, sugarcane (*Saccharum officinarum*) was introduced by the British to Barbados and by the French to St. Kitts in the 1640s (Watts 1995). The crop adapted well to all but the driest parts of the Caribbean, but its agronomic demands posed sweeping environmental consequences for the region. Intolerant of competition for sunlight, water, and nutrients, cane could be successfully grown only by clear-cutting the native forest and weeding continuously. Lowland zones provided the best soil and nutrient combinations for cane cultivation, and consequently these areas were most extensively cleared to make way for the crop. Soon the only areas remaining under forest cover were the highland zones of mountainous islands, such as St. Lucia, Dominica, and the other Windwards, where steep slopes precluded plantation agriculture. Yet even higher elevations were not entirely spared the effects of cane cultivation, for the boilers used to refine sugar were usually fueled by firewood cut from upland forests. In comparison, the more low-lying Leeward islands were rapidly stripped of all forest cover to accommodate cane cultivation. In Barbados, virtually all of the island's seasonal forests had been cut and replanted with cane by 1665, within just twenty years of English settlement. St. Kitts, Nevis, and Montserrat followed suit by the 1680s; Antigua, Guadeloupe, Martinique, and lowland Jamaica by the 1750s; and the Spanish territories of Santo Domingo, Cuba, Puerto Rico, and Trinidad were almost entirely devoted to cane by the end of the eighteenth century.

The ecological consequences of sugarcane cultivation in the Caribbean would be difficult to overstate. It is estimated that thousands of plant and animal species were driven to extinction in this process (Watts 1985). On Barbados, writers of the 1650s commented on the marked absence of songbirds compared to other islands. By that time all forest-dwelling birds, other than several hummingbird species, had disappeared together with their habitats (1985:273). The region's shift to a monocrop plantation economy also accentuated ecological problems as varying metropolitan demands for sugar dictated cultivation practices and intensity. When European markets became glutted with sugar or prices fell, Caribbean planters typically fallowed some of their land, opening a niche for other plant species on their farms. Since the native forest cover had been eliminated, more often than not these niches were filled by weed species introduced (usually unwittingly) from abroad. The legacy of this pattern is an extraordinarily high level of nonnative plant species found on most of the islands of the Caribbean. On Barbados, 88.7 percent of the wild plant species recorded in the 1960s originated from outside the island, one of the highest levels of nonnative vegetation of any country in the world (1985:275).

The clearing of native forest and cultivation and harvest of sugarcane required vast quantities of human labor, a vexing problem for colonists witnessing the extinction of native populations. The demand for agricultural labor was resolved in the sixteenth century by the Atlantic slave trade: over the ensuing 250 years an estimated 1.7 million Africans were transported to Britain's Caribbean holdings alone (Richardson 1983). The presence of African slaves and demand for plantation land quickly swallowed up the small-scale tobacco and subsistence farms earlier established by European yeoman farmers. On the sugar-growing islands, African populations soon vastly outnumbered European settlers. Because of the sheer size of the workforce required for cane production (on St. Kitts, for example, the slave population by the late 1700s reached 360 per square mile) and the devotion of virtually all arable land to sugarcane, the Caribbean came to rely heavily on imported food (Richardson 1996).

As slaves, plantation workers in the Caribbean subsisted from a precarious mix of crops cultivated on kitchen gardens supplemented by food rations imported from Britain. If these arrangements were disrupted, as they were when low metropolitan sugar prices forced planters to curtail food imports, slaves suffered malnutrition, high child mortality, and occasional famine. At such times they were exhorted to produce even greater amounts of agricultural wealth, which, in Mintz's words, "flowed into the European metropolises in great rivers, nourishing infant industry . . . and supporting the growth and spread of culture and civilization" (1964: xvi). Environmental injustice in the Caribbean, historically, was not felt in the polluting byproducts of manufacturing plants, but in the cruel ironies of plantation economies that compelled workers to their greatest expenditures of labor at precisely those times when they suffered the greatest restrictions in their dietary intake. The root of this injustice, of course, was the monopolization of island land for sugar production rather than for the subsistence needs of those who worked it. The parallel with environmental racism in the southern United States is unmistakable; in both cases, the benefits of economic growth accrued elsewhere while environmental costs were borne disproportionately by people of African descent. Emblematic of this process was the distribution not only of land in the Caribbean but all vital resources required by the islands' populations. For example, sugar plantations intercepted the water supplies destined for urban populations and diverted them to water-driven mills for crushing cane. After a piped water system was installed in Kingstown, St. Vincent, in the 1880s, residents had access to water for just one half hour per day because upstream plantations diverted most of it.

POSTEMANCIPATION PARADOXES

Abolition occurred throughout the British West Indies in 1838, but it did little to ameliorate such injustices, for the end of slavery was nowhere associated with a redistribution of land. Tied to plantation work by dearth of alternatives, former slaves were subjected as well to a long-term decline in the viability of sugar production. As yields fell due to soil exhaustion and the British market became saturated with beet sugar from continental Europe, plantation economies throughout the West Indies entered a protracted depression in the 1880s. None bore the effects of this crisis more heavily than the black workforce. By the following decade, hunger and sheer economic desperation had reached explosive proportions throughout the eastern Caribbean, creating paradoxes in living standards and land use reminiscent of Steinbeck's *Grapes of Wrath*. Thus, the best farmlands in flat, lowland zones were owned by sugar planters yet were left idle because of low prices, generating mass unemployment among plantation workers. Nor did the growing ranks of the unemployed enjoy access to uncultivated lands for their own use in the highlands. Since the advent of the Byres Plan on St. Vincent in 1766, highland zones adjacent to plantations that were themselves unfit for cane cultivation were allotted to planters to discourage any economic independence on the part of plantation workers (Richardson 1996). This pattern of land monopolization as a mechanism of labor control was common throughout the postemancipation Caribbean (Bolland 1981). Even as infant mortality rates soared from food shortages on Barbados and the Windward Islands, colonial administrators refused to release lands to unemployed workers from a fear that, in the words of St. Lucia's governor Gouldsbury, land grants would "relieve [the worker] of the stern necessity of continuous daily toil" (quoted in Richardson 1996:160). It took a wave of protracted civil unrest over the deepening misery of the plantation workforce for the British government to appoint a Royal Commission of Inquiry into conditions in the Caribbean in 1897. Recognizing the volatility of the situation and eager to create a politically stable class of small farmers, the commission recommended the sale and distribution of Crown lands to former sugar workers (Lobdell 1988). This process eventually led to the dismantling of the great sugar estates and a redistribution of the region's land resources among a "reconstituted peasantry" (Mintz 1984). By the time of the Commission of Inquiry, planters had long ceased to enjoy political support in London, for free-trade policies embraced by the British government favored sugar from Cuba and continental Europe priced at just a fraction of the Barbadian and Windwards product.

FROM AGRICULTURE TO TOURISM: CONTEMPORARY CARIBBEAN LANDSCAPES

On lands that once yielded sugar for the British market, West Indian smallholders turned to other export crops throughout the twentieth century. In the post–World War II period, as the Caribbean faced decolonization amid uncertain economic prospects, the British government actively promoted banana production for export among the region's small farmers. By the 1990s, some forty thousand farmers in the Windward Islands of St. Lucia, St. Vincent, Dominica, and Grenada were producing bananas, mostly for shipment to the United Kingdom. Unique among the world's banana industries, fruit production in the Windwards is almost exclusively the domain of small, family-owned farms. Compared to corporate-owned farms in Central and South America, which often comprise thousands of acres each, the large majority of Windward Island farms are fewer than ten acres in size. Accordingly, most earnings from the Windwards banana industry have accrued to local families rather than to the shareholders of metropolitan-based banana companies. Since its introduction in the 1950s, banana farming is credited with vastly improving the incomes and standards of those living on the islands (Grossman 1998). At present, however, the future of the eastern Caribbean banana industry appears bleak, at best. In 1998, acting at the behest of the U.S. government and the U.S.-based Chiquita corporation, the World Trade Organization ordered the dismantling of marketing privileges that Caribbean bananas have long enjoyed in the European Union (see Raynolds 2003 for discussion of this ruling). The current trading regime will not end until 2006, but it remains to be seen whether some form of marketing preference that is compliant with the WTO ruling can be maintained after that date. In the meantime, the uncertainties awaiting farmers in the coming years have already fueled an exodus from the industry. On islands such as St. Lucia, an estimated 84 percent of banana farmers who were commercially active in the early 1990s had abandoned the industry by 2003 (La Force, personal communication 2003).

Having exhausted their challenges to the WTO mandate, governments in the region are now urging "marginal" banana farmers to find employment in other sectors. The major legal alternative to banana farming is tourism. Yet this sector has failed to absorb most of the rural residents displaced from banana production, nor do its wages approach the earnings formerly enjoyed by banana producers. For many former banana growers and workers, drug trafficking and production provide much more attractive alternatives to the meager wages and indignities of tourism employment. By the mid-1990s, marijuana production had surpassed bananas as the largest source of agricultural income on St. Vincent, which is now second only to Jamaica as the Caribbean's largest marijuana producer (*Business Focus* 1995:8). Despite the illegal status of the crop, its producers on St. Vincent have recently organized a Marijuana Growers Association (patterned after the island's Banana Growers Association) to lobby for their interests and regulate the industry. There are also some indications that what remains of the region's banana industry is being increasingly harnessed to the illegal drug trade. On several occasions in recent years, boxes of bananas originating in St. Lucia were found upon arrival in the United Kingdom to contain millions of dollars worth of cocaine (*Voice* 2002:1). Given that only a small percentage of the banana boxes comprising each shipment are opened for inspection in England, the magnitude of such trafficking must be considerably larger than what is indicated by such accidental discoveries.

As the region shifts from an equitable and environmentally sustainable economic strategy built on smallholder banana farms to heavier reliance on tourism, it is almost certain to incur the social and environmental costs experienced elsewhere (Conway 2002). In older sites of Caribbean tourism, such as Barbados and Antigua, these environmental consequences have degraded the very resources that once attracted hundreds of thousands of visitors per year to each destination (Pattullo 1996b). The construction of beachfront resorts has decimated mangrove swamps and coastal wetlands throughout the region. Antigua, for example, witnessed the loss of 50 percent of its mangrove coastline over a fifteen-year period beginning in 1980 (1996b). Coastal wetlands are essential for mitigating water pollution and rainwater runoff, especially in places lacking modern sewage treatment facilities. Further, they are critical to the tourist industry itself in providing nurseries for the reef fish and lobsters that island-based hotels and restaurants rely upon for much of their sales (Sasidharan and Thapa 2002). Divers and marine biologists working in Antigua and Barbados confirm that the effect of coastal tourist development has been siltation of once-pristine inshore waters, dying coral reefs, and dwindling fish stocks.

The Caribbean's heavy involvement in cruise ship–based tourism has also aggravated problems of water quality and waste disposal while contributing little employment or revenue to the islands. On St. Lucia in any recent year cruise ships have accounted for the majority of all tourist arrivals, yet they have generated less than 10 percent of all tourism revenues (*Voice* 2003:2). Attempts by island governments to capture their revenue potential by imposing head taxes and environmental levies usually lead cruise operators to simply remove the offending islands from their itineraries. Often constructed with substantial subsidies from the governments of their home countries, luxury cruise ships offer travel packages that significantly undercut land-based operations in terms of price. Their employment contributions to island economies are limited to the several thousand Caribbean residents who work on board cruise ships and to the vendors who hawk handicrafts and T-shirts to passengers at each port of call. On board, Caribbean cruise ship workers encounter an apartheid-like division between themselves and the lighter-skinned, usually European employees who work in higher-paid and tipped positions.

While almost all profits on cruise ship tourism are repatriated, the ships leave in their wake a host of environmental and waste disposal problems. Worldwide, cruise ships discharge 20 million gallons of raw sewage into the seas every day (Ioannides 2002) and leave behind huge volumes of solid waste. Waste disposal from cruise ships and land-based hotels has joined coastal water quality as the most significant environmental problem on small, densely populated islands where landfill space is at a premium. On Barbados, the government created a new landfill in the mid-1990s largely to deal with the waste generated by the four hundred thousand or more visitors to the island each year (Beckles 1996). Ironically, the dump is situated in the middle of one of the few remaining forested places on the island, a national park that the government has also promoted as a significant ecotourism attraction. In older sites of Caribbean tourism such as Barbados and Antigua, the effects of environmental degradation were already being felt by the late 1980s as growing numbers of tourists abandoned both islands for less environmentally compromised destinations.

One place less affected is St. Lucia, formerly the largest banana-producer among the four Windward Islands. The dawning of mass tourism on the island began in 1989 with the planned construction of the Jalousie Plantation Resort and Spa. This foreign-owned, sixty-million-dollar resort was to be built on a 320-acre site between the two peaks of the Pitons, the steep volcanic cones that are the country's most recognizable natural feature (France 1998). The development plans at what was considered a treasured national landmark triggered opposition among many St. Lucians and at the Organization of American States, which recommended preservation of the site as a national park. Notwithstanding public protests and international appeals, the St. Lucian government authorized the project as a means of generating foreign exchange and employment. Some environmental costs of the resort were apparent even before its opening, as rainwater runoff damaged a nearby reef and artifacts from an Amerindian burial site were destroyed in the building of tennis courts. Jalousie is an all-inclusive resort, following a model pioneered by Club Med in which tourists prepay for their rooms, meals, drinks, and entertainment and are encouraged, in the words of the Sandals resort chain, to "leave [their] wallets at home." All-inclusives are controversial because they virtually seal off their guests from any contact with local people. What contact does occur is strictly regulated. At Jalousie, local fishermen are no longer permitted to work in coastal waters within sight of sunbathing guests, and nonguests can only enter the resort or use an ostensibly public beach after having purchased an expensive pass. Restrictions on access to all-inclusives provoked widespread indignation in the Caribbean after an incident in 1994 when Lester Bird, the prime minister of Antigua, was barred from entering a resort on that island because he lacked a pass (Pattullo 1996a:82). As prepaid, foreign-owned enterprises, all-inclusives generate few of the economic linkages to the local community that are present in traditional tourist operations. In St. Lucia, eight of the country's twelve major hotels are foreign-owned all-inclusives that repatriate virtually all of their profits, generating palpable resentment among local restaurant owners, tour guides, cab drivers, and vendors (Pattullo 1996a).

During the course of a year, approximately twice as many people visit St. Lucia as reside on the island. Land values have soared from a boom in resort and condominium construction, which has accelerated the exodus from agriculture. Meanwhile, many of the problems of sewage and waste disposal experienced in "mature" tourist destinations such as Barbados and Antigua are repeating themselves on St. Lucia. During a conference on water management in October 2002, foreign technicians toured several projects designed to address these problems on the island. Among them is the Deglos Landfill, a site designed for the solid waste from hotels and cruise ships. There were audible gasps from the group of geologists and engineers when they learned that the landfill sat atop a pressure point on the island's largest aquifer, which provides drinking water for the forty-five thousand residents of Castries and irrigation for hundreds of banana farms.

As agriculture recedes in the wake of the WTO ruling, tourism is left standing as one of the few legal sources of economic activity available to the eastern Caribbean. The shift from smallholder farming to tourism seems likely to reverse a century-long trend of greater equity in resource use that began with the Royal Commission of 1897. On Barbados, where tourists use 4 times as much electricity, 10 times as much fresh water, and generate

1.5 times as much solid waste as local residents, the foreign exchange and employment benefits of tourism have clearly come at high cost with regard to resource use. Unlike that island, where much of the tourist infrastructure remains in the hands of Barbadians, the foreign-owned, hermetically sealed enclaves of all-inclusive resorts on St. Lucia compound profligate resource use with an exceptionally limited distribution of economic benefits. Indeed, their restrictions on public access to facilities and beaches, which are frequented almost exclusively by white guests, strike even the most casual observer as the relic of an earlier era from the Deep South. It is in this sense that the environmental justice paradigm resonates with the Caribbean, whose patterns of resource use and development are reverting to an earlier pattern of foreign ownership and inequality. As Tim Hector, an opposition politician and journalist on Antigua, has observed: "In the beginning, a tiny, foreign elite in ownership and management controlled sugar. In the end a tiny, foreign elite in ownership and management controls tourism. Throughout our history, slavery or wage-slavery that has been our lot" (quoted in Pattullo 1996a:65).

ACKNOWLEDGMENTS

Research on St. Lucia has been supported by the National Science Foundation, grant BCS 0003965. The author thanks Tawnya Sesi Moberg for her collection of data on banana farming and resource use on the island in October and November 2002.

REFERENCES

Allen, B. 2003. *Uneasy Alchemy: Citizens and Experts in Louisiana's Chemical Corridor*. Cambridge: MIT Press.

Beckles, H. 1996. Where Will All the Garbage Go? Tourism, Politics, and the Environment in Barbados. In *Green Guerrillas: Environmental Conflicts and Initiatives in Latin America and the Caribbean*, ed. H. Collinson, 187–94. London: Latin American Bureau.

Bolland, O. 1981. Systems of Domination after Slavery: The Control of Land and Labor in the British West Indies after 1838. *Comparative Studies in Society and History*. 23(4):591–619.

Bullard, R. 1990. *Dumping in Dixie: Race, Class, and Environmental Quality*. Boulder: Westview Press.

———. 1996. Environmental Justice: It's More than Waste Facility Siting. *Social Science Quarterly*. 77:493–499.

Business Focus. 1995. Is Castries the Money-Laundering Capital of the OECS? *St. Lucian Business Focus* 2(2):8–9.

Conway, D. 2002. Tourism, Agriculture, and the Sustainability of Terrestial Ecosystems in Small Islands. In *Island Tourism and Sustainable Development*, ed. Y. Apostolopoulos and D. Gayle, 113–30. Westport, Conn.: Praeger.

Di Chiro, G. 1992. Defining Environmental Justice: Women's Voices and Grassroots Politics. *Socialist Review* 22:93–130.

Dowie, M. 1995. *Losing Ground: American Environmentalism at the Close of the Twentieth Century*. Cambridge: MIT Press.

Erikson, K. 1994. *A New Species of Trouble: Explorations in Disaster, Trauma, and Community*. New York: Norton.

France, L. 1998. Sustainability and Development in Tourism on the Islands of Barbados, St. Lucia and Dominica. In *Resource Sustainability and Caribbean Development*, ed. Duncan F. M. McGregor, D. Barker, and S. Evans. Kingston, Jamaica: Press University of the West Indies.

Grossman, L. 1998. *The Political Ecology of Bananas: Contract Farming, Peasants, and Agrarian Change in the Eastern Caribbean*. Chapel Hill: University of North Carolina Press.

Ioannides, D. 2002. Tourism Development in Mediterranean Islands: Opportunities and Constraints. In *Island Tourism and Sustainable Development*, ed. Y. Apostolopoulos and D. Gayle, 67–92. Westport, Conn.: Praeger.

La Force, H. 2003. Personal communication. August 13. Cul-de-Sac, St. Lucia.

Las Casas, B. 1992 [1552]. *The Devastation of the Indies: A Brief Account*. Trans. H. Briffault. Baltimore: Johns Hopkins University Press.

Lentz, D. 2000. *An Imperfect Balance: Landscape Transformations in the Precolumbian Americas*. New York: Columbia University Press.

Lobdell, R. 1988. British Officials and the West Indian Peasantry, 1842–1938. In *Labour in the Caribbean: From Emancipation to Independence*, ed. M. Cross and G. Heuman. London: Macmillan Caribbean.

Mintz, S. 1964. Foreword to *Sugar and Society in the Caribbean: An Economic History of Cuban Agriculture*, by R. Guerra y Sanchez. New Haven: Yale University Press.

———. 1984. *Caribbean Transformations*. Baltimore: Johns Hopkins University Press.

———. 1985. *Sweetness and Power: The Place of Sugar in Modern History*. New York: Viking.

Moberg, M. 2001. Co-opting Justice: Transformation of a Multi-racial Environmental Coalition in Southern Alabama. *Human Organization* 60(2):166–77.

———. 2004. Caribbean. In *Encyclopedia of World Environmental History*, vol. 1, ed. S. Krech III, J. R. McNeill, and C. Merchant, 190–95. New York: Routledge.

Patullo, Polly. 1996a. *Last Resorts: The Cost of Tourism in the Caribbean*. London: Latin American Bureau.

———. 1996b. Green Crime, Green Redemption: The Environment and Ecotourism in the Caribbean. In *Green Guerrillas: Environmental Conflicts and Initiatives in Latin America and the Caribbean*, ed. H. Collinson. London: Latin American Bureau.

Raynolds, L. 2003. The Global Banana Trade. In *Banana Wars: Power, Production, and History in the Americas*, ed. S. Striffler and M. Moberg. Durham: Duke University Press.

Richardson, B. 1983. *Caribbean Migrants: Environment and Human Survival on St. Kitts and Nevis*. Knoxville: University of Tennessee Press.

———. 1996. *Economy and Environment in the Caribbean: Barbados and the Windwards in the Late 1800s*. Gainesville: University Press of Florida.

Sasidharan, V., and B. Thapa. 2002. Sustainable Coastal and Marine Tourism Development: A Hobson's Choice? In *Island Tourism and Sustainable Development*, ed. Y. Apostolopoulos and Dennis J. Gayle. Westport, Conn.: Praeger.

United Church of Christ. 1987. *Toxic Wastes and Race in the United States: A National Report on the Racial and Socio-economic Characteristics of Communities with Hazardous Waste Sites*. New York: United Church of Christ Commission for Racial Justice.

Voice. 2002. Drugs in Our Banana Boxes. *St. Lucia Voice*. December 7. 114(8854):1.

Voice. 2003. SLHTA President Blasts Cruise Sector. *St. Lucia Voice*. May 24. 115(8908):2.

Watts, D. 1995. Ecological Responses to Ecosystem Shock in the Island Caribbean: The Aftermath of Columbus, 1492–1992. In *Ecological Relations in Historical Times*, ed. R.A. Butlin and N. Roberts, 267–79. Oxford: Blackwell.

Contributors

Paul Farnsworth is Associate Professor of Anthropology, Department of Geography and Anthropology, Louisiana State University. His research interests include colonial and postcolonial archaeologies of the Caribbean and the American South and West. He is editor of *Island Lives: Historical Archaeologies of the Caribbean* and coauthor with Laurie A. Wilkie of *Sampling Many Pots: An Archaeology of Memory and Tradition at a Bahamian Plantation.*

Faye V. Harrison is Professor of African American Studies and Anthropology at the University of Florida. Her research interests include noncanonical histories of anthropology, Caribbean and Caribbean diaspora, the U.S. South, the impact of global restructuring and neoliberal policies on the economic strategies and political practices of the urban poor, and the human rights implications of race and gender intersections. She recently edited and contributed to *Resisting Racism and Xenophobia: Global Perspectives on Race, Gender, and Human Rights* and is completing a book on critically reconstructing anthropology from the vantage point of raced and gendered "outsiders within."

Rosalyn Howard is Assistant Professor of Anthropology and Director of North American Indian Studies at the University of Central Florida. Her research interests focus on the African diaspora in the Caribbean and include Native American and African interrelationships, ethnohistory, and cultural identity. Her most recent publication is "Yoruba in the British Caribbean: A Comparative Perspective of Trinidad and the Bahamas," in *The Yoruba Diaspora in the Americas.*

Joyce Marie Jackson is Associate Professor of Anthropology at Louisiana State University. Both a folklorist and an ethnomusicologist, she is currently completing a book on African American sacred quartets. She is the author of *Life in the Village: A Cultural Memory of the Fazendeville Community*. She also conducts research on performance-centered rituals in

Africa and the African diaspora and on the rural roots of jazz in southern Louisiana.

Mark Moberg is Professor of Anthropology, Department of Anthropology and Sociology at the University of South Alabama in Mobile. His research interests center on the anthropology of work, the environment, globalization, and agricultural change. He is the author of *Myths of Ethnicity and Nation: Immigration, Work and Identity in the Belize Banana Industry* and coeditor of the volume *Banana Wars: Power, Production, and History in the Americas.*

Helen A. Regis is Associate Professor of Anthropology at Louisiana State University. Research interests include neoliberalism, citizenship, and colonial memory in Africa and the African diaspora. She is the author of *Fulbe Voices: Marriage, Islam, and Medicine in Northern Cameroon* and coauthor with John Bartkowski of *Charitable Choices: Religion, Race, and Poverty in the Post-welfare Era.* She is writing an ethnography of race, memory, and public space in New Orleans.

Christopher P. Toumey is Centenary Research Associate Professor of Anthropology, University of South Carolina. He is the author of *God's Own Scientists: Creationists in a Secular World* and *Conjuring Science: Scientific Symbols and Cultural Meanings in American Life.*

Martha Ward is University Research Professor of Anthropology and Urban Studies at the University of New Orleans. Her most recent book is *Voodoo Queen: The Spirited Lives of Marie Laveau.* In the aftermath of Hurricane Katrina, she is continuing her research on the Voodoo community, the culture of hurricanes, and the public culture of New Orleans.

Laurie A. Wilkie is Associate Professor of Anthropology at the University of California, Berkeley. Her research interests include archaeologies of identity, difference, and personhood in the recent past. She is the author of *The Archaeology of Mothering: An African American Midwife's Tale,* winner of the 2005 James Deetz Prize, awarded by the Society for Historical Archaeology. She has more recently coauthored *Sampling Many Pots: An Archaeology of Memory and Tradition at a Bahamian Plantation* with Paul Farnsworth.